# BLITZKRIEG

**Below:** A column of Cruiser Mk.IV tanks of 5th RTR prepare for action near Quesnoy on 30 May 1940. On the bow of the lead vehicle can be seen the yellow and black bridging circle in the right corner, the unit code in the centre and the divisional rhinoceros insignia to the left. (I.W.M., London)

# BLITZKRIEG

## Armour Camouflage and Markings, 1939-1940
### Steven J. Zaloga

a&ap

Arms & Armour Press
London–Melbourne

*To Nicholas, Coleen and Tony.*

# CONTENTS

Published by
Arms and Armour Press,
Lionel Leventhal Limited,
2-6, Hampstead High Street,
London NW3 1QQ,
and at
4-12, Tattersalls Lane,
Melbourne, Victoria 3000.

British Library Cataloguing in Publication Data:
Zaloga, Steven
Blitzkrieg
1. Armoured vehicles, Military—Camouflage
2. Armoured vehicles, Military—Markings
3. World War, 1939-1945—Supplies
I. Title
355.8'3        UG446.5

ISBN 0-85368-334-4

Colour artwork by Steven J. Zaloga
Edited by Tessa Rose.
Designed by Anthony A. Evans.
Typeset by Trade Linotype Limited, Birmingham.
Printed and bound in Great Britain by Fakenham
Press Limited, Fakenham, Norfolk.

**Right:** A Pz.Kpfw. 38(t) of Pz.Rgt.25, 7.Panzer Division on
exercise near Blévy after the Battle of France, clearly shows
the divisional insignia immediately behind the cross insignia
on the hull. The turret numbers are probably red and white.
(National Archives, Washington, DC)

| GLOSSARY | | | | | | |
|---|---|---|---|---|---|---|
| English | Dutch | French | German | Italian | Polish | Russian |
| division | divisie | division | division | divisione | dywizja | diviziya |
| brigade | brigade | brigade | brigade | brigata | brygada | brigada |
| regiment | regiment | regiment | regiment | reggimento | pułk | polk |
| battalion | bataljon | bataillon | abteilung | bataglione | batalion | batal'on |
| company | compagnie | compagnie | kompanie | compagnia | kompanja | rot |
| squadron | eskadron | escadron | schwadron | squadroni | szwadron | eskadron |
| platoon | peleton | peleton | zug | plotoni | pluton | vzvod |
| troop | sectie | section | zug | truppa | dywizjon | vzvod |

# PREFACE

This book examines the camouflage painting and insignia used on armoured vehicles of the combatant powers during the campaigns at the beginning of the war in Europe in 1939 and 1940. As it is aimed primarily at the serious historical modeller, several technical matters should be discussed. It has long been accepted dogma in the hobby community that a replica should be finished in precisely the same shade of paint that was used on the original vehicle. This seems logical enough, and has led to proliferation of paint chips, authentic colour mixes and so on. Unfortunately, it ignores the important size difference between a real tank and a 1/76 or 1/35 scale replica and the resultant visual discrepancy. The perception of colour by the human eye varies between large and small objects: a replica, if painted in exactly the same shade as the full-size original, will appear to be distinctly darker. To test this yourself, when you next visit an army exhibition, take with you a colour chip of the current camouflage colour. If you stand about one hundred feet away from a vehicle freshly painted in the same colour as the chip, you will notice that the small chip appears darker than the vehicle. Place the chip on the vehicle, and they will match. The complex reasons for this discrepancy have been dealt with in more detail in a number of articles, especially Ian Huntley's 'A Question of Scale Colour'.

This is not to suggest that precise knowledge of the original camouflage colour is not needed, to the contrary. But merely painting a replica in the same shade as the original will not suffice. One argument, perennially heard at modelling conventions where a competitor's model has been criticized by a judge for use of inaccurate colours, is that there is no such thing as a true colour since the actual paint used varied due to erratic quality control, improper mixing and the effects of natural weathering. This is true to a point, but does not justify the use of colour at the whim of each individual modeller. An olive green paint may vary, with a slightly more yellowish tint in one batch and a slightly more brownish tint in another, however this hardly justifies the use of a colour such as garish grass green.

The effect of natural weathering is a complex process dependent upon the stability of the pigment and solvent, on weather conditions and on the amount of abuse the surface is subjected to. A careful eye towards the effect of weathering on painted machinery in everyday situations, such as in a railway yard, will help the modeller master this technique in finishing his replica. For example, in many types of paint, yellow is a far less stable pigment than red oxide. Therefore, it looks quite strange on a replica to see a bright and vivid ochre shade

Below: A Panzerspähwagen (Sd.Kfz.232) followed by a leichte Panzerfunkwagen (Sd.Kfz.223) pass through a French village in June 1940. The leading armoured car has few markings apart from the national insignia, while the radio car following has a licence plate, the Guderian group 'G' sign, the stencilled rectangle for Aufklärung Abteilung 57 and, below this, the inverted 'Y' with two dots, insignia for 6.Panzer Division. (National Archives, Washington, DC)

Opposite page: The R-35 infantry tank was the most numerous tank type of the French Army in 1940. This vehicle is finished in a pattern of ochre and olive green. The military matricule (50133) can be seen under a heavy coat of dust, and on the turret is the name Simoun in white. (E.C.P.A., Paris)

when the neighbouring patches of olive green and rust brown are dull and faded.

The colour illustrations here are not intended to be perfect representations of their subject. All of the illustrations are carefully based on photographs, but, in most cases, the amount of weathering and dirt shown on the upper hulls of the tanks has been kept to a minimum so as not to obscure small details of markings or camouflage patterns.

Tank camouflage and insignia are of very little concern to the soldier in the field. Military records on the subject are few and far between, and many have been lost over the years. Unlike aircraft camouflage, which was fairly uniform owing to the common practice of standardized, factory-applied patterns and colours, tank camouflage was usually the responsibility of each individual unit, with only the most general guidelines provided by headquarters; the same applies to markings. Therefore, when referring to camouflage and marking practices, it should be kept in mind that invariably there were exceptions to the rule. Attrition rates of tanks in combat were very high, and replacement tanks brought up from reserves were unlikely to be marked similarly to other vehicles in the unit.

The dearth of official documents on these subjects means that photographic interpretation must serve as a major source of information. There are inherent limits to such a source owing to the limited supply of good quality photographs and the lack of adequate captioning. Some units are covered in great detail while virtually nothing exists for other units. The task of ferreting out rare and interesting photographs takes years of patient effort, and is only now beginning in this field. I would like to acknowledge my appreciation for the efforts of those pioneers, and their articles and books, on which I have relied, are listed in the Bibliography. Several people have kindly helped in the preparation of this book, and I would like to extend my personal thanks to them. To Janusz Magnuski, for his generous help on the Polish section; David List on the British section; Fred Vos on the Dutch section; Pierre Touzin on the French and Belgian sections; and Tom Jentz, Bruce Culver, Lee Ness and George Balin on the German section. I would also like to thank the staffs of several of the archives I visited in the course of my research, especially Messrs. Rolland and Guillaume of E.C. P. Armée, Paul White of the National Archives, the staff of the photographic library of the Imperial War Museum, and Vika Edwards and Robin Roseman of Sovfoto.

Steven J. Zaloga, 1980

# INTRODUCTION
## The Genesis of Tank Camouflage

The use of pattern-painted camouflage on military equipment became widespread during the Great War. The advent of breech-loaded, rifled artillery made small, precise targets vulnerable to direct fire from considerable ranges. Coupled with the birth of reconnaissance aircraft, the need for concealment grew apace. The most sophisticated efforts in camouflage were usually undertaken by the artillery branch, since static gun positions were particularly vulnerable to aerial bombardment and counter-battery fire. The fact that the positions were static provided camouflage teams with more options, as elaborate nets and natural foliage could be used.

The new armoured vehicles posed a trickier problem. Their large size and angular shapes made them ill-suited to concealment in natural cover, even one so shattered and ravaged as the front line trench areas. Elaborate nets and foliage combinations were only practical when the vehicles were immobile in rear areas before an assault. Once they moved, nets were a hindrance and a potential hazard to running gear and moving parts. Pattern-painted camouflage, while no panacea to this problem, was better than nothing. Two trends were evident. The British Royal Tank Corps eventually settled upon what can be called the utilitarian finish: a simple monotone scheme in a dark, matt paint (by the end of the war, a dark green). The rationale behind this was that elaborate pattern-painted camouflage, as used at Cambrai in 1917, soon became so encrusted with mud as to be indistinguishable. Obvious or not, it probably did little good since a tank in motion is all too apparent to its adversaries; the glint of steel tracks, the exhaust fumes, noise and the cloud of dust it raises are all tell-tale signs.

The other approach, best exemplified by the French, stressed disruptive, geometrically intricate pattern-painted camouflage. Unlike the British rhomboids, the French tanks were not so prone to plastering themselves in mud. The French realized that the greatest threat to their tanks was the long-range fire of German field-guns. A tank was most vulnerable when at a halt — perhaps due to mechanical breakdown, an obstruction, or to fire its gun — and the ragged geometric patterns blended well with the torn-up terrain of the Western Front, thus serving to momentarily confuse the German gunners.

The German approach was to use less elaborate, mimetic camouflage. Three natural colours — ochre, green and brown — were applied in irregular, ill-defined blotches.

Paradoxically, the purpose of insignia is diametrically opposite to camouflage, for it identifies rather than conceals. Distinctive national insignia may prevent troops from shooting at their own tanks, but it also alerts the enemy, and can provide a good aiming point. In fact, excessively conspicuous markings can defeat the whole purpose of the camouflage. During the Great War, the French shied away from any prominent display of national insignia on their tanks, though both British and German tanks carried them boldly. The crews of all the nations added a host of smaller markings, either to identify their vehicles within a unit or to personalize their machines with a name or cartoon, but they were usually too small to affect the camouflage.

After the war, disruptive pattern-painting generally gave way to utilitarian monotone finishes. Vehicles looked sharper for parades and inspections, and, of course, it cost less money. In many countries it was the custom to rub oil or varnish over the matt paint for parades, which gave a glossy finish but ruined what little value the paint may have had as camouflage.

**Below:** Bren Carriers of 2nd Battalion, Royal Inniskilling Fusiliers moving through Chapel St. Aubin where they were billeted as GHQ troops during the BEF's assembly period at Le Mans. The striped camouflage is particularly curious. There is little in the way of markings on the vehicles aside from the civilian licence plates and four-digit mobilization number on the right mudguard of each vehicle. (I.W.M., London)

# BELGIUM

The Belgian armoured force, although small, used some of the most unique equipment seen in the early months of the Second World War. However, divided up amongst the infantry and cavalry formations, it had little impact on the course of the conflict.

Belgian tanks were uniformly painted in 'kaki', a colour resembling the later American olive drab. There are a few photographs showing vehicles of the 3e Lanciers with a sprayed-on camouflage of unknown colours, but this was a rare exception to the rule. The national insignia was displayed in two forms: a tricolour in black, yellow and red on the serial block, and a small tricolour roundel. The serial block was a black rectangle with the tricolour to the extreme left and a four-digit number in white. Positioning of the markings was as follows.

## T.13 Type I
Type I carried a roundel on the semi-turret sides and sometimes had a company number painted on the upper rear corner of the foldable side plate armour. The serial was carried centrally on the lower bow plate in the front and on the upper left of the rear plate.

## T.13 Type II
The Type II serving with the infantry usually had the roundel on the hull sides. Those serving with cavalry units often had the roundel on the turret with the regimental insignia in white above it. The serial was carried in the same place as on the Type I.

## T.15
The T.15 carried the roundel on the turret with the

Top: A column of Belgian Vickers Utility tractors move to the front towing 47mm FRC anti-tank guns. These diminutive vehicles were used in large numbers to tow anti-tank guns and other loads for Belgian infantry and cavalry regiments. The roundel can barely be seen on the forward part of the hull side, but the military matricule is clearly visible. (E.C.P.A., Paris)

Bottom: This column of T.15s display no regimental markings on their turrets, but the national roundel is evident in the usual place. (Author's Collection)

**Opposite page, top:** A pair of T.15 light tanks with white cloth bands around their turret tops as manoeuvre markings during training in the Phoney War period. The tank on the left clearly displays a four-digit military matricule preceded by a national tricolour. (Author's Collection)

**Below left:** A trio of Belgian T.15 light tanks under review. They carry the raging bull insgnia of the 2e Regiment de Chasseurs à Cheval. Slightly above this insignia is the Belgian roundel. (Joseph Desautels)

**Right:** A T.13 Type III is abandoned by the roadside. On the turret, a white unicorn's head is painted; the unit to which this sign belonged is unknown. The military matricule is missing, though the rectangular mounting frame at the upper left corner of the hull is still in position. The T.13 used a semi-turret with a completely exposed rear, as is evident from this view. (National Archives, Washington, DC)

**Below right:** A T.15 of 3e Regiment de Lanciers rests unarmed in a depot beside two T.13 Type III. The regimental sign, a death's head, can be seen above the national roundel. The military matricule on the nearest T.13 has been painted-out. (National Archives, Washington, DC)

| Order of battle of major Belgian armoured sub-units, 10 May 1940 | | | | |
|---|---|---|---|---|
| Unit | | T.13 | T.15 | ACG-1 |
| 1e | Division d'Infantrie | 12 | | |
| 2e | Division d'Infantrie | 12 | | |
| 3e | Division d'Infantrie | 12 | | |
| 4e | Division d'Infantrie | 12 | | |
| 7e | Division d'Infantrie (R) | 12 | | |
| 8e | Division d'Infantrie (R) | 12 | | |
| 9e | Division d'Infantrie (R) | 12 | | |
| 10e | Division d'Infantrie (R) | 12 | | |
| 11e | Division d'Infantrie (R) | 12 | | |
| 1e | Division des Chasseurs Ardennais | 48 | 3 | |
| 2e | Division des Chasseurs Ardennais | | 3 | |
| Compagnie Ind. de l'Unité Cyclistes Frontière | | 12 | | |
| 8e | Companie de l'Unité Cyclistes Frontière | 12 | | |
| Compagnie PFL de l'Unité de Forteresse | | 12 | | |
| 1e | Division de Cavalerie | | | |
| | 1er Regiment de Guides | 6 | 6 | |
| | 2e Regiment de Lanciers | 6 | 6 | |
| | 3e Regiment de Lanciers | 6 | 6 | |
| 2e | Division de Cavalerie | | | |
| | 1er Regiment de Lanciers | 6 | 6 | |
| | 1er Regiment de Chasseurs | 6 | 6 | |
| | 2e Regiment de Chasseurs | 6 | 6 | |
| Escadron d'Auto-Blindées | | | | 8 |

regimental insignia above it in white. In pre-war manoeuvres, many T.15s had exercise markings consisting of a white band extending several inches along the upper edge of the turret. Serials were carried in the usual places.

## ACG-1

Initially, ACG-1s were left in their original French markings, which consisted of three-digit white numerals (in the 800 block) on the hull front and sides. Before the war these had been overpainted and replaced by more conventional serial blocks on the right front mudguard and on the left rear plate. The roundel was carried on the turret. Some of these Renaults carried the bison head insignia on the front of the turret.

## Tracteur Chenille

These diminutive tractors were used in large numbers by infantry units. Their markings usually consisted of a roundel on the side and serials at both front and rear.

The illustrations in this section show a variety of cavalry insignia commonly used on the tanks of the Belgian Army. The affiliation of some of these signs is not known.

**Opposite page, top:** An interesting close-up of the turret of a T.13 Type III shows a very elaborate turret painting as well as the national insignia. The identity of this unit is unknown. (Pierre Touzin)

**Opposite page, bottom:** An ACG-1 of the Escadron d'Auto-Blindées, believed to be that of Lt. Schreiber, commander of one of the platoons that took part in the battle at Kwatrecht on 20 May 1940. The military matricule is carried on the mudguard. By the time of the campaign, the squadron's colourful rhinoceros head insignia had been painted over on many tanks of the unit. (National Archives, Washington, DC)

**Right:** A Utility tractor carrying a group of infantry. On the tractor's side panel is an inscription with the unit's name and the crowned trumpet sign used by Belgian light infantry regiments. Unfortunately, the inscription is too small to be legible. (National Archives, Washington, DC)

# FRANCE

The French Army indulged in some of the most lavish and colourful tank markings of all the combatant powers. Unfortunately, research on this fascinating subject has been far more limited than that on the Wehrmacht or BEF, in part because of the loss of much of the relevant archival material; with the exception of François Vauviller's excellent essay in Pierre Touzin's book *Les Engins Blindés Français, 1920-1945 Vol. I* there is little in print. It is, therefore, with some trepidation that general rules on the subject should be laid down. This is all the more true since French tank markings were not strictly regulated by the Grand-Quartier-General as they were by the High Commands of most other countries. The responsibility for markings was often left to regimental commanders.

## Camouflage Painting

In 1930, the French Army prepared a provisional set of instructions on camouflage techniques. In their view, camouflage was "the art of concealing troops and organization by whatever means available from enemy observation, or to counteract the effects of this observation". Of the eighty pages devoted to the subject, only one dealt with provisions for using paint as camouflage and it is worth quoting.

"There are two cases to consider in the camouflage of equipment: protection against close observation, or against medium and long-range observation. Against short-range observation, it is suitable to examine the camouflage of combat tanks and cavalry armoured cars. This camouflage is obtained by means of irregular blotches of paint laid in such a fashion as to create false contours for aiming. In this manner, it is difficult for the enemy to discern the actual contours. Against medium and long-range observation, these blotches are to be avoided because they produce no such illusion. In addition, photographs taken from an aeroplane at normal observation heights reveal, in most cases, the presence of equipment by the shadows they cast; the colour has no effect. Generally, equipment which is painted grey-blue or olive green appears as white in photographs taken with ordinary photographic plates. The roofs of vehicles also appear white, in spite of their colour, because the surface reflects. As of this moment, the regulation paint for equipment is matt olive green (vert olive mat) except for metal pontoon bridge boats which are to be painted matt grey-black."

French armoured vehicles were amply provided with nets and other similar static camouflage equipment, but these were unsuitable for mobile operations.

By the mid-1930s, the use of multi-colour camouflage had come into vogue again. This camouflage was occasionally applied by units in the field, but, more

Below: The Char Lourd 2C was by far the largest tank of the campaign, and was an outgrowth of experiences in the Great War. Six of these vehicles served with 51e BCC, but all were attacked by Stukas and destroyed on a freight wagon near the Marne before they could see action. This photograph shows pre-war markings, plus the name Alsace and the vehicle number. During the war they were renumbered in the 90-99 range. All were finished in overall dark olive green. (E.C.P.A., Paris)

**Top:** There were a surprisingly large number of these antiquated FT-17s still in service in 1940, though they were held in reserve. This pair served with 29e BCC in the 2e Armée sector. The tail of the second vehicle can be seen in the lower left corner, and on it the club and circle insignia of 1e compagnie, 4e section. The camouflage is ochre and dull brown. (E.C.P.A., Paris)

**Middle:** The early French types, such as Char D2 and Char B1, were often factory-painted in very elaborate schemes, and this D2 is no exception. This vehicle has not yet entered service and has no markings, but clearly shows a typical two-tone ochre and olive green camouflage pattern. (Joseph Desautels)

**Bottom:** Vehicle markings were left to battalion commanders, and ranged from non-existent to quite elaborate, as in this case. All these vehicles, believed to be of 12e BCC, have different white markings on the turret sides. In this photograph can be seen white circles, chevrons and double bars. The camouflage scheme is a horizontal three-tone scheme edged in black. (E.C.P.A., Paris)

often than not, it was applied at the factory; a practice that led to certain similarities in pattern between certain types of vehicles.

Besides the basic colour of olive green (also called 'kaki mat', vert armée', etc.) there were two other basic camouflage colours used by the French Army. Ochre was used either as a camouflage colour or to outline the other two colours. It varied from a light sienna to a fuller, dry mustard colour. A dark chestnut brown was also commonly used. Black was frequently used to outline the other colours. All three tones could be utilized in a number of fashions: monotone olive green; two tone, generally green and ochre; three tone; two tone with outlines, either olive green with ochre outlined in black, or olive green with brown outlined in ochre or black; three tone outlined in black.

As was the case in most peacetime armies, the monotone green vehicles were sometimes varnished or polished with oil to give a gloss finish for inspection or parades. When war broke out, these had to be completely repainted. At the beginning of 1940, armoured units were ordered to paint their vehicles in overall 'vert ou gris armée' (army grey or army green). This directive was largely ignored in regards to vehicles already in service, but often new factory-supplied vehicles were left in monotone green or grey. The grey was a blue-grey somewhat lighter than German grey. There are reports of vehicles painted in multitone grey patterns, but this has not been confirmed. In some

units, it was the practice to use a form of dichotomous camouflage on squadron commanders' tanks. Generally, this consisted of painting the hull in the usual green and ochre with black outlines, but finishing the turret in ochre with black outlined blotches. This practice was seen most frequently on Somua and Hotchkiss armoured fighting vehicles, but was not very common.

## National Insignia

All French tanks carried national tricolours. Usually they were very small and appeared at the front and rear, preceding the matricule (serial). On some vehicles, such as the Char B, they were carried in additional places. While most units refrained from using the more conspicuous national roundels, others, especially cavalry units, frequently painted them on the upper or rear surfaces. After the outbreak of the war, the practice became more widespread, for reasons that will be made apparent by the following anecdote. On 19 May 1940, Char Bs of the 46e BCC of the newly-formed 4e DCR came under fire from Somuas of the 3e Cuirassiers, causing many casualties. To prevent a recurrence, an officer went to find some paint to apply roundels. This unfortunate gentleman was almost summarily executed as a looter, since he lacked the correct requisition form, but several hours and a good many francs later he returned, and the unit painted roundels on the front, rear, flanks and roof of each vehicle.

Below: Units of De Gaulle's 4e DCR are shown here on the march in the spring of 1940. The Char D2 to the right, belonging to 2e compagnie, 4e section, 19e BCC has shed a track. Note that the company sign on the turret covers the remains of a vehicle name beginning 'TO–'. The R-35 probably belongs to 24e BCC. Apart from the matricule, a very dirty white circle insignia can be seen on the bow directly above the oval plate denoting the manufacturer. (E.C.P.A., Paris)

**Right:** King George VI inspects a group of R-35, possibly of 43e BCC, in the 3e Armée sector behind the Maginot Line. The tanks are finished in olive green and dull brown, with the pattern outlined in ochre. Each tank carries a name on the right super-structure front and on the left side of the turret. On the right side of the turret is a large number 4. Some names used were Le Terrible, Frompe la Mort, Buffle. (E.C.P.A., Paris)

**Below:** This R-35 served with 12e BCC and had the white geometric sign, in this case two vertical bars, peculiar to the unit. The camouflage pattern is an intricate mixture of ochre, brown and olive green blotches outlined in black. The small white grenade bridging sign can be seen on the tool-box over the mudguard. (E.C.P.A., Paris)

**Top:** An R-35, unit unknown, which fought against 3.Panzer Division near St. Père on 12 June 1940. The vehicle is painted in three-tone colours and has the name Jaguar on the turret. The broad, sweeping camouflage pattern is not particularly common to the R-35. (National Archives, Washington, DC)

**Middle:** This particular H-35 of 4e Cuirassiers also appears in the colour plates. The roundels are quite evident in this overhead view, as are the turret numbers and the regimental crest—Joan of Arc on a red shield. (E.C.P.A., Paris)

**Bottom:** H-39s from an unidentified cavalry regiment take part in an inspection. Interestingly, the vehicle numbers are split on the rear of the turret, though on the sides both digits appear together. Below the military matricule can be seen a small tricolour. These vehicles are finished in overall olive green. (E.C.P.A., Paris)

**Opposite page, top:** A section of H-39s take part in manoeuvres. The section chief is flying a flag to identify his position. The vehicles are named L'Impeccable and L'Impassable and carry the vehicle number on the turret sides and probably on the rear as well. The colour scheme is probably overall olive green, though it may be the later army grey. (E.C.P.A., Paris)

**Opposite page, bottom:** Two independent companies of H-39 were sent to Norway during the fighting there: the 342e and 351e Compagnies Autonomes. Here, a rather cosmopolitan group comprising French, British and Polish troops sit and chat. The H-39s in Norway carried little in the way of markings aside from a matricule. Some had names chalked on the turrets when they embarked from France, but these were removed on arrival in Norway. The finish is overall olive or army grey. (I.W.M., London)

## Regimental Insignia

Some French armoured units, particularly cavalry regiments, carried colourful regimental insignia on the sides of their vehicles. Not all of these signs are known, but a number of them are shown in the photographs and illustrations. They were usually based on the regimental badges worn on dress occasions.

## Tactical Insignia

Certainly the marking most commonly associated with French tanks is the so-called playing card symbol. These symbols were derived from the insignia used by the tanks of the Artillerie Speciale groups in the Great War. They were not true card symbols, but consisted of card symbols placed on white, geometric shapes. The geometric design indicated the company, while the card design indicated the section. The system was as follows:

| | |
|---|---|
| 1st Company | Circle (35cm diameter) |
| 2nd Company | Square (30cm side) |
| 3rd Company | Triangle (45cm base, 40cm height) |
| | |
| 1st Section | Spade |
| 2nd Section | Heart |
| 3rd Section | Diamond |
| 4th Section | Club |

The card symbol was painted in blue for the 1st battalion and red for the 2nd battalion.

Due to the differences in organization between 1918 and 1940, the First World War symbols were seldom used in their complete form. It was common to see only the card symbol without the geometric-pattern backing, particularly in cavalry units. Similarly, it was possible to see just the company geometric symbol, as in the case of Char Bs. In some units, the marking was amplified further by the addition of a number or design within the card symbol to identify the regiment.

Besides using these insignia, two other forms of tactical markings were also common on French tanks. Large turret numbers were often used in cavalry formations. Cavalry 'escadron' (squadrons) usually consisted of twenty tanks or armoured cars divided into four 'peleton' (platoons) with five vehicles each. Therefore, the numbering could take the form of 1 to 20 or, by platoon, 1-5, 10-14, 20-24 and 30-34, but there were several variations. In the Division Légère Mécanique, there were two mixed regiments with forty Hotchkiss and forty Somuas. These formed four 'escadron' with a total of sixteen 'peletons'. The numbering in these units was continuous, 10-90, as tanks have been seen with numbers as high as 89.

In many Char B battalions, the 'chef de section' (section chief) would choose a letter, sometimes the first initial of his last name, and this would be adopted by the three tanks of his section. This is covered in greater detail below.

## Names

French armoured vehicles often bore names. Generally, these were applied on a standardized basis, usually a whole battalion at a time. The practice was most common with Char B, Char D2 and Hotchkiss, and details of the systems used are explained below. While most names were patriotically inspired, some were more lighthearted; as in the case of the 4e escadron of the 2e GRDM, which used such names as Drolesse and Gauloise.

## Serial Numbers

All French armoured vehicles were given serial numbers (matricules). These were issued in blocks to the factories, so certain patterns are evident. The systems are summarized below for some of the more common

**Opposite page, top:** A group of H-39/40 are prepared for shipment in the spring of 1940. These vehicles are finished in a sprayed pattern of ochre, brown and olive green. Markings would be applied on arrival to their unit. (National Archives, Washington, DC)

**Opposite page, middle:** Not all H-39s served with the cavalry. This H-39 belonged to 25e BCC and was disabled during fighting with 7.Panzer Division near Avesnes. The turret marking is in red and white, while the vehicle is finished in overall dark olive green. (National Archives, Washington, DC)

**Opposite page, bottom:** This Char B1 bis shows the markings typical to these vehicles. On the turret side and hull flank is the section letter 'S'. The name Var is on the side of the turret. The company symbol is on the turret rear but, as the door is open, this cannot be seen. It is quite evident from the caked-on mud covering the hull side why the flocage camouflage was not adopted for the Char B1. (E.C.P.A., Paris)

**Top right:** Char B1 bis (355) Bourgueil shows the usual positions of markings on the hull front and turret. Note the tricolour under the vehicle name. The vehicle number is carried on the bar beneath the main gun, but is barely visible due to accumulated grime. Near the turret visor, a small heart can be seen. This style of marking was not common on the Char B1 bis. The dividing line between the olive green and ochre paint on the turret is very evident. (E.C.P.A., Paris)

**Bottom right:** Char B1 bis (257) Bourrasque carries a number of untypical but interesting markings. This tank belonged to 8e DCR and was captured near Montcornet in May 1940 after experiencing engine problems exacerbated by trying to recover two other broken-down Char B1s. The yellow lion above the name on the hull front is unique and probably a personal marking of the crew. A large red and white heart insignia can be seen on the left turret side, and this was repeated on the left turret rear. (I.W.M., London)

**Top:** Char B1 bis Eclair shortly after disembarking from the railway station at d'Etain. This was the tank of Captain Deyber, seen riding on the turret door, who was the commander of 2e compagnie of 8e BCC. He chose the first letter of his own name for the section letter. In front of this can be seen the company sign, a white square, usually positioned on the side. The camouflage is painted in green and ochre with the pattern outlined in black. (E.C.P.A., Paris)

**Middle:** Char B1 bis (330) Cher belonging to 37e BCC at Beaumont, Belgium on 16 May 1940. A white square with a red spade on the turret rear indicates that it was from 2e compagnie, 1e section. It was unusual for Char B units to use a section sign, such as the spade, since the same function was served by the large letter marking. The vehicle number (330) was carried on the right side door as seen here, as well as on the hull front. (Author's Collection)

**Bottom:** Char B1 bis of 2e section, 1e compagnie, 37e BCC, knocked-out near Mettet in Belgium on 15 May 1940. This view clearly shows the full set of markings carried on many Char Bs. The section letter can be seen on the turret side and is repeated on both corners of the hull rear. The company and section signs, a white circle with a red heart within, are carried on both sides of the turret rear. Barely evident at the top of the letter 'U' on the right side is the vehicle number (467). (E.C.P.A., Paris)

types of vehicles. For example, on R-35s the number was invariably five digits and began with '5'. These numbers were applied at the factory and were generally preceded by a national tricolour, and occasionally by the prefix 'M' ('militaire') as well. The sequence was M-Tricolour-serial. On some vehicles, such as the Somua S-35 and Panhard 178, no pattern is evident, and on the infantry's prolific UE tractor, there were so many built that they took up all five-digit blocks from 30000 to 90000 left over from other armoured vehicles. The serial number was sometimes painted directly over the camouflage in the case of a monotone green vehicle, but on many camouflaged vehicles it was painted on over a thin black rectangle.

**Serial blocks issued to common vehicle types**

| Tank | Number | Serial block |
|------|--------|--------------|
| Char 2C | two digits | 90-99 |
| Char B | three digits | 101- |
| Char D2 | four digits | 2001- |
| FCM 36 | five digits | 30001-30090 |
| P-16 | five digits | 37000- |
| H-35/39 | five digits | 40001- |
| R-35/39/40 | five digits | 50001- |
| AMR 35 | five digits | 90001- |

## Marking Patterns
Many of the marking and camouflage patterns were peculiar to certain types of vehicles, so it is worthwhile briefly summarizing features for the major vehicle types.

### Char léger 17R (FT-17)
There were a surprisingly large number of these antiquated vehicles on hand in 1940, and many retained their First World War-style markings. The camouflage

tended to be of a two-tone variety in horizontal swatches. Card markings were typical, with the battalion number sometimes painted in white on the card symbol. Serial numbers, both a redundant 1918 serial and a more recent number, were carried on the hull side and on the suspension girder.

### Char léger 35R (R-35, R-39, R-40)
R-35s were usually camouflaged in a two- or three-tone scheme using small blotches outlined in black or ochre. The later R-39 and R-40 generally remained in monotone green. Card symbols were often used, but usually without the geometric company portion of the insignia. Names were seldom carried and, indeed, R-35s were relatively plainly marked as compared to most other French tanks. Some of the more elaborate and colourful markings can be seen in the colour illustrations, but it should be remembered that for every colourfully marked R-35, there were several more with no markings to speak of, aside from the serial and bridging marks. The bridging symbol was always carried on the sides of the tool boxes on the mudguards.

### Char léger 35H and 38H and Char de cavalerie H-35 and H-39.
The Hotchkiss was unique in serving with both infantry tank battalions and 'escadrons' of the cavalry. Therefore, its markings reflected the simplicity of the infantry tanks and the more colourful practices of the cavalry. The infantry Hotchkiss frequently were left in monotone dark green and their markings were fairly plain, similar to those of the R-35. Card symbols were the most elaborate markings carried. In contrast, the cavalry H-35s and H-39s often carried regimental badges, turret numbers, roundels and other designs, and were frequently painted in multi-coloured camouflage.

**Below:** An advancing column of H-35s belonging to 3e section, 18e Dragons, 1e DLM. The regimental marking, a hippogriff on a red diamond edged in white, can barely be seen on the turret side. At the rear is a very prominent roundel and vehicle number. The camouflage scheme is olive green with ochre blotches edged in black. (E.C.P.A., Paris)

Late production H-39/40s were sometimes spray-painted in three-tone schemes.

### Char Moyen D1 and D2

All Char D1 battalions were stationed in North Africa. The 67e BCC returned to France in June 1940, and this battalion's tanks were painted in a monotone dark green and carried no markings. In contrast, the D2 was rather colourfully marked. It was generally finished in a two-tone scheme of green and ochre with black outlines. Certainly the most famous of the D2 units was 19e BCC, which served with De Gaulle's 4e DCR. Before the war, De Gaulle had ordered that the tanks be marked with the names of famous battles of the Great War. These names were carried on the hull front and both sides of the turret until the outbreak of the Second World War when the latter were overpainted with card symbol insignia. The 19e BCC also carried the white disc symbol peculiar to tanks of 4e DCR. This marking was carried on the front and rear of the vehicle, but its purpose is unclear. It was also carried on the R-35s of 4e DCR.

### Char léger FCM 36

The FCM 36 was used by only two battalions, 4e and 7e BCC. It was invariably painted in an intricate horizontal three-tone pattern. Typically, the vehicles' serials were painted on black rectangles. Some of the FCM 36 of 7e BCC carried a blue and white insignia depicting a tank gunner. Other FCM 36 carried a solid white square, possibly the marking of 2e compagnie, 4e BCC. A few FCM 36 were named, e.g. Le Mistral (30001) — such names were painted on the upper edge of the mantlet.

### Char B

The Char Bs were certainly the most elaborately marked tanks of the 1939-40 battles. Few other tanks have carried so complicated a set of markings. The most common style of camouflage on the early Char B1s was olive green with ochre outlined in black. It was painted on in a very intricate fashion which, for lack of a better phrase, could be described as resembling a plucked grape stem. The subsequent Char B1 bis carried less complex patterns, but were just as colourful. Without a doubt, the most elaborately painted of these was Fantasque (No. 251). In December 1939 an engineer by the name of Marc Marchal, who was president of the French chemists and would be a tanker himself in 1940, proposed a new type of camouflage called 'flocage'. This was obtained by spraying fine fibrous filaments onto a tank previously painted with a gummy type of paint. Fantasque, a Char B1 bis of 8e BCC, was used for the experiment. First, the tank was painted with a special mixture of glue and green paint and, while still dry, the fibre was sprayed on. Many colours were used, ranging from maroon for tree trunks and limbs to greens and yellows for simulated leaves. The final result resembled a small stand of trees. Trials conducted alongside Char B Alpes in ordinary paint resulted in the scheme being dropped. While the textured surface worked quite well in reducing reflections off the armour, it was very expensive and time-consuming to apply. More importantly, it was found that, after a few hours of running cross-country, the fibre became so coated with dirt as to be unrecognizable.

The matricule on the Char B was displayed in two and sometimes three places: on the bar immediately below the 75mm gun at the front, in the centre of the access door on the right side of the hull, and sometimes on the upper left corner of the rear hull plate.

All Char B1 and Char B1 bis of the initial production batches up to machine 431 were given names in a systematic fashion. The system used to allot these names is summarized below, and samples of the names are given where known. After machine 431, names were issued more irregularly. In some units, replacement vehicles from these new batches were christened after older vehicles, such as Vendée II and Verdun II. Others were never named.

The name was carried on the hull front below the driver's visor and on the right and left sides of the turret. A national tricolour was carried below it on the hull front, and also beneath the name on the right side of the turret but not on the left.

It was the practice in some Char B battalions to use a letter, usually chosen by the section chief, for each section of three vehicles. This was carried on the turret sides, at the rear of the hull sides, and on both corners of the rear plate. Occasionally, the insignia consisted of both a letter and a number, such as 3A or 4A, but this was not as common.

The Char B battalions used geometric symbols to distinguish companies. In contrast to the customary card symbol marking, the geometric signs on the Char Bs were usually hollow. On some vehicles, the card symbol itself was used within a hollow geometric sign, but this does not show up well in photographs. These geometric signs were carried on both sides of the turret rear. In 41e BCC, a small solid geometric sign was painted on the turret side.

**System of allocating names to vehicles in Char B units**

| Type | Matricule | Theme | Unit | Sample Names |
|------|-----------|-------|------|--------------|
| B1 | 101-135 | Provinces | 37e BCC | Bourgogne (121), Reims (107) |
| B1 bis | 201-235 | Provinces, colonies, towns | 15e BCC | Marseilles (234), Madagascar (206) |
| B1 bis | 236-270 | Destroyers and torpedo-boats | 8e BCC | Typhon (266), Sirocco (263) |
| B1 bis | 271-305 | Towns and colonies | 28e BCC | |
| B1 bis | 306-345 | Rivers | 41e and 49e BCC | Durand (322), Cher (330) |
| B1 bis | 346-375 | Wines | 41e and 49e BCC | Mercurey (347), Pommard (343) |
| B1 bis | 376-387 | 1914–18 victories | 41e and 49e BCC | Vauquois (377), Beni Snassen (387) |
| B1 bis | 388-410 | 1914–18 victories | 46e and 47e BCC | Arlay (388), Craonne (391) |
| B1 bis | 411-431 | Military leaders | 46e and 47e BCC | Mal. Petain (414), Foch (411) |

**Below:** A Somua S-35, probably of 1 DLM, in the usual three-tone horizontal colour scheme with a red and white 1e section spade insignia. A vehicle number seems to be lacking on this Somua. (I.W.M., London)

**Left:** Somua S-35 of 4e section, 18e Dragons. Like most Somuas, when a regimental sign was carried, it was usually painted on the hull side. In this case, it consists of a white club with a red or blue circle containing a white hippogriff. The vehicle matricule is 67252. (Joseph Desautels)

**Below left:** Somua S-35 of the 4e Cuirassiers with the regiment's red and white Joan of Arc marking on the hull side. This vehicle is finished in the common three-colour pattern of horizontal swathes frequently seen on late-production Somuas. The vehicle number and a roundel can be seen on the turret. (E.C.P.A., Paris)

## Char Lourd 2C

The behemoth Char 2C served only with 51e BCC, and these were knocked-out on their railway wagons before seeing action. They carried a two-digit number on the front of their sponsons. At least one was hastily camouflaged, but most were left in overall dark green.

## Char de cavalerie 35S (Somua S-35)

The S-35 served with six of the cavalry regiments. The early production lots were painted in the three-tone scheme with black outlines and patterns in the vertical style. Later batches used a distinctive pattern of horizontal swatches. Turret numbers were carried on the sides of the turret, with a roundel at the rear and sometimes on top. When the regimental insignia was carried, it was generally found on the front sides of the hull. Card symbols, when used, were carried on the front sides of the turret but were without the geometric company designation.

## AMR 33/35

The AMR reconnaissance tanks were usually finished in a three-tone scheme. The early machines had a hard-edged finish, but colours on later vehicles were often

outlined with black sprayed on with an airbrush, leaving a feathered edge. These vehicles carried the squadron numbers on the rear turret sides and a roundel on the back of the turret. Regimental insignia were often carried.

## Armoured Cars

The cavalry's armoured cars, such as the P-16 half-track and Panhard P-178 were seldom camouflaged. Markings usually consisted of squadron numbers carried on the rear turret sides, and a roundel on the turret rear. Regimental insignia were common on the P-16 and were usually carried on the bonnet side, but were rarely seen on the P-178.

## Tracteur UE

The UE was the most numerous armoured vehicle of the 1940 campaign on either side. They were invariably finished in overall olive green, and markings seldom amounted to more than the matricule and an occasional bridging sign. Between the two crew domes was a plaque with a blue square and yellow triangle painted on it. This was carried pointing forward to indicate that the tracteur UE was towing a trailer or other load.

## Miscellaneous Markings

On some infantry vehicles, especially the R-35 and the UE tractor, a bridging class sign was painted. This was a white grenade with a black bridging class number 1. Sometimes this sign was yellow.

Owing to the lack of radios on most French tanks, communication between them was carried out by flares or flags. The pennion of the section chief was red with a white horizontal band, the sub-officer's was red with a white vertical stripe, and the last member of the section carried a blue one with a white vertical stripe. All tanks also carried a yellow flag to signal distress.

**Order of battle of major French armoured units, 10 May 1940** [1]

| Unit | R-35 | H-35 | H-39 | FCM 36 | D2 | B1 | 2C | FT-17 |
|---|---|---|---|---|---|---|---|---|
| 1e Division Cuirassé | | | | | | | | |
|   25e BCC | | | 45 | | | | | |
|   26e BCC | | | 45 | | | | | |
|   28e BCC | | | | | | 35 | | |
|   37e BCC | | | | | | 33 | | |
| 2e Division Cuirassé | | | | | | | | |
|   8e BCC | | | | | | 35 | | |
|   14e BCC | | | 45 | | | | | |
|   15e BCC | | | | | | 35 | | |
|   27e BCC | | | 45 | | | | | |
| 3e Division Cuirassé | | | | | | | | |
|   41e BCC | | | | | | 35 | | |
|   42e BCC | | | 45 | | | | | |
|   45e BCC | | | 45 | | | | | |
|   49e BCC | | | | | | 35 | | |
| 4e Division Cuirassé | | | | | | | | |
|   2e BCC | 45 | | | | | | | |
|   19e BCC | | | | | 45 | | | |
|   24e BCC | 45 | | | | | | | |
|   44e BCC | 45 | | | | | | | |
|   46e BCC | | | | | | | 25 | |
|   47e BCC | | | | | | | 25 | |
| Bataillons Organiques | | | | | | | | |
|   1e BCC | 45 | | | | | | | |
|   3e BCC | 45 | | | | | | | |
|   4e BCC | | | 45 | | | | | |
|   5e BCC | 45 | | | | | | | |
|   6e BCC | 45 | | | | | | | |
|   7e BCC | | | 45 | | | | | |
|   9e BCC | 45 | | | | | | | |
|   10e BCC | 45 | | | | | | | |
|   11e BCC | | | | | | | | 63 |
|   12e BCC | 45 | | | | | | | |
|   13e BCC | | 45 | | | | | | |
|   16e BCC | 45 | | | | | | | |
|   17e BCC | 45 | | | | | | | |
|   18e BCC | | | | | | | | 63 |
|   20e BCC | 45 | | | | | | | |
|   21e BCC | 45 | | | | | | | |
|   22e BCC | 45 | | | | | | | |
|   23e BCC | 45 | | | | | | | |
|   29e BCC | | | | | | | | 63 |
|   30e BCC | | | | | | | | 63 |
|   31e BCC | | | | | | | | 63 |
|   32e BCC | 45 | | | | | | | |
|   33e BCC | | | | | | | | 63 |
|   34e BCC | 45 | | | | | | | |
|   35e BCC | 45 | | | | | | | |
|   36e BCC | | | | | | | | 63 |
|   38e BCC | | 45 | | | | | | |
|   39e BCC | 45 | | | | | | | |
|   40e BCC | 45 | | | | | | | |
|   43e BCC | 45 | | | | | | | |
|   48e BCC | 45 | | | | | | | |
|   51e BCC | | | | | | | 6 | |
| Bataillon Coloniale (Armée des Alpes) | | | | | | | | 63 |
| Compagnie Autonome de Chars | | | | | | | | |
|   342e Cie A | | 15 | | | | | | |
|   343e Cie A | | | | | | | | 10 |
|   344e Cie A | | | | | | | | 10 |
|   345e Cie A | | | | 15 | | | | |
|   346e Cie A | | | | 15 | | | | |
|   347e Cie A | | | | | 11 | | | |
|   348e Cie A | | | | | 11 | | | |
|   349e Cie A | | | | | 11 | | | |
|   350e Cie A | | | | | | | | 10 |
|   351e Cie A | | 15 | | | | | | |
|   352e Cie A | | | | | 11 | | | |
|   353e Cie A | | | | | 11 | | | |

| Cavalry formations | H-35 | H-39 | S-35 | P-178 | AMR |
|---|---|---|---|---|---|
| 1e Division Légère Mécanique | | | | | |
|   4e Cuirassiers | 40 | | 40 | | |
|   18e Dragons | 40 | | 40 | | |
|   6e Cuirassiers | | | | 40 | |
|   4e Dragons | | | | | 60 |
| 2e Division Légère Mécanique | | | | | |
|   13e Dragons | 40 | | 40 | | |
|   29e Dragons | 40 | | 40 | | |
|   8e Cuirassiers | | | | 40 | |
|   1e Dragons | | | | | 60 |
| 3e Division Légère Mécanique | | | | | |
|   1e Cuirassiers | | 40 | 40 | | |
|   2e Cuirassiers | | 40 | 40 | | |
|   12e Cuirassiers | | | | 40 | |
|   11e Dragons | 60 | | | | |
| 1e Division Légère de Cavalerie | | | | | |
|   1er RAM | 12 | | | 12 | |
|   5e Dragons | | | | | 20 |
| 2e Division Légère Mécanique | | | | | |
|   2er RAM | 12 | | | 12 | |
|   3e Dragons | | | | | 20 |
| 3e Division Légère de Cavalerie | | | | | |
|   3er RAM | 12 | | 3 | 12 | |
|   2e Dragons | | | | | |
| 4e Division Légère Mécanique | | | | | |
|   4er RAM | 12 | | | 12 | |
|   14e Dragons | | | | | 20 |
| 5e Division Légère de Cavalerie | | | | | |
|   5er RAM | 12 | | | 12 | |
|   15e Dragons | | | | | 20 |
| 1e GRDI (1 DIM) | | | | 12 | 20 |
| 2e GRDI (2 DIM) | 20 | | | 12 | |
| 3e GRDI (3 DIM) | | | | 12 | 20 |
| 4e GRDI (9 DIM) | | | | 12 | 20 |
| 5e GRDI (12 DIM) | 20 | | | 12 | |
| 6e GRDI (15 DIM) | | | | 12 | 20 |
| 7e GRDI (25 DIM) | | | | 12 | 20 |

1. Figures do not include sizeable French tank units in North Africa and the Levant, or depot and training tanks.

| Abbreviation | French | English |
|---|---|---|
| BCC | Bataillon de Chars de Combat | Tank battalion |
| Cie. A | Compagnie Autonome de Chars | Independant tank company |
| DCR | Division Cuirassé | Armoured division |
| DIM | Division d'Infanterie Mécanique | Mechanized infantry division |
| DLC | Division Légère de Cavalerie | Light cavalry division |
| DLM | Division Légère Mécanique | Light mechanized division |
| GRDI | Groupe de Reconnaissance de Division d'Infanterie | Reconnaissance group of an infantry division |
| RAM | Régiment Auto-Mitrailleuses | Armoured car regiment |

**Above:** There were several thousand of these tiny tracteur UEs in service with the French Army in 1940. They were finished in overall olive green, and the only markings were the matricule on the bow and the convoy sign between the two crew domes, indicating that the tractor was towing a trailer. This sign consisted of a blue plate with yellow triangle and is clearly evident in this photograph. (E.C.P.A., Paris)

**Left:** Panhard P-178 armoured cars were usually plainly marked and, unlike this one, left in overall dark olive green paint. Close examination of the glacis plate reveals a pattern of dull brown and green with black outlines. The contrast between these three colours in a black and white photograph is very poor, and it is difficult to determine the pattern. The name and lightning bolt insignia are personal markings. (E.C.P.A., Paris)

# GERMANY

## Camouflage Painting

The handful of A7V tanks manufactured by Germany in the Great War were mostly finished in a mimetic pattern consisting of a base coat of ochre with ill-defined blotches of dark green and chestnut brown. The Versailles Treaty of 1919 limited the Reichswehr to a few armoured cars for police duty. The experimental tanks clandestinely built and tested at the secret Kazan training station in the Soviet Union appear to have used the same colours, but with sharply defined edges in most cases. During Reichswehr training manoeuvres, dummy tanks fabricated from canvas and plywood over commercial car frames were used to simulate armoured attacks. These were often camouflaged in the same three-tone, hard-edged mimetic pattern. With the Nazis' rise to power in 1933, the secret tank programmes slowly surfaced. Many of the early Pz.Kpfw.1s were camouflaged in the three-tone mimetic pattern with either the hard edge or feathered edge finish. After 1935, a simpler two-tone scheme was introduced, with dark grey as the base colour and a dark brown applied in patterns over it. The proportion of the colours was supposed to be one-third brown to two-thirds grey, and could be applied either with a spray gun or by brush. On many vehicles, the brown colour was never applied. By the outbreak of the war in September 1939, the bulk of the Wehrmacht's armoured vehicles were in the drab, monotone dark grey. The exclusive use of dark grey as an economy move for the duration of the war was officially mandated in an army directive, HM 1940 No. 864 on 31 July 1940, but it is clear from photographic evidence that this practice had been in effect for some time.

The grey adopted by the Wehrmacht was a very dark grey with a slightly bluish tint. In sunlight, it became a chalkier, lighter shade. The grey was so dark, in fact, that Pz.Kpfw.Is serving with the Condor Legion in Spain were popularly called 'negrillos' ('the black ones'). The adoption of this colour is perplexing. Dark grey was ostensibly chosen to make the vehicle blend better in the shadow of buildings or trees, where it was supposed to be parked when not mobile. Yet a dark brown or green are equally effective in such settings and are more natural in other surroundings whether forested or open. It is speculative, but entirely possible, that the grey was chosen as a subtle means of national identification, similar to the attempt by most nations to adopt a standard infantry uniform colour and design that would be distinctive and unmistakable. As Germany's likely foes (France, Britain, Poland and Belgium) relied on various shades of dark green as their predominant vehicle colour, grey would serve this function.

The Wehrmacht's lack of interest in vehicle camouflage at this stage of the war reflected the offensive tenor of German tactics. Tanks were designed for brisk advance and, when in movement, were nearly impossible to conceal, no matter how elaborate the camouflage paint. When at rest, sensible dispersal of

**Below:** A leichte Panzerfunk-wagen (Sd.Kfz.223) of 7.Panzer Division assigned to a Luftwaffe forward air controller to co-ordinate air attacks for the division. The usual Wehrmacht Heer licence was painted over and replaced by the Wehrmacht Luftwaffe code letters. Next to this can be seen the divisional sign. Also evident is a prominent white swastika insignia on the bow. (E.C.P.A., Paris)

**Above:** Pz.Inz.222 half-tracks were available in small numbers in 1939 and were intended for the motorized cavalry regiments. The three-tone sprayed paint finish on this example is very evident on the sides of the rear compartment. (Janusz Magnuski)

**Right:** This Panzerfunkwagen (Sd.Kfz. 263) 6-rad on pre-war manoeuvres was finished in the two-tone brown and grey scheme. There is very little contrast between these colours, and the pattern is only evident on the cloth spare wheel cover. The stencilled marking on the right mudguard is curious in that it contains the sign for both the Nachrichten (signals) and Panzerspähwagen (armoured car) units. The lettered code below 'AA4' indicates Aufklärung Abteilung 4 (Reconnaissance Battalion 4), which served with 1.Panzer Division. The licence plates are in the standard positions. Barely evident on either side of the 'WH' on the plates are the small, red Feldpost numbers. (National Archives, Washington, DC)

**Top:** A Pz.Kpfw.II Ausf.B of 5.Panzer Division knocked-out in the fighting with the Polish 6th Infantry Division around Pszczyna on 2 September 1939. The crosses have been overpainted in yellow, but the number remains in white. Below the number is a rhomboidal band of yellow, black, yellow, which may have been used to distinguish Pz.Rgt.15 from Pz.Rgt.31. (National Archives, Washington, DC)

**Middle:** A Pz.Kpfw.I Ausf.B knocked-out at Pszczyna, probably by a mine. The markings are a yellow cross, white numbers and a yellow, black, yellow band. Note that the cross was carried in four positions on the turret. (National Archives, Washington, DC)

**Bottom:** A column of 4.Panzer Division advances along a rain-swept road, trailed by a klein Panzer Befehlswagen (light command tank). The markings on these vehicles have been obscured by grime. The cross is barely evident on the left hull rear. On the rear of the cupola is the division's three-pointed star insignia, and to the left of the silencer is the vehicle sign 'RO2'. (National Archives, Washington, DC)

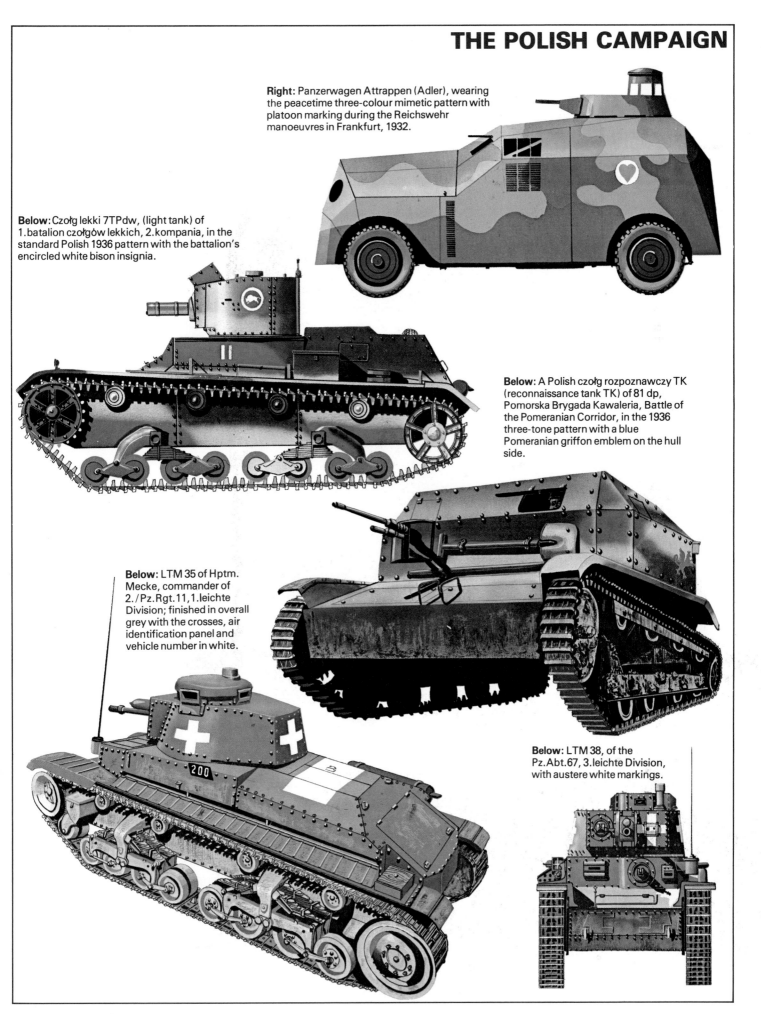

**Right:** Panzerwagen Attrappen (Adler), wearing the peacetime three-colour mimetic pattern with platoon marking during the Reichswehr manoeuvres in Frankfurt, 1932.

**Below:** Czołg lekki 7TPdw, (light tank) of 1.batalion czołgów lekkich, 2.kompania, in the standard Polish 1936 pattern with the battalion's encircled white bison insignia.

**Below:** A Polish czołg rozpoznawczy TK (reconnaissance tank TK) of 81 dp, Pomorska Brygada Kawaleria, Battle of the Pomeranian Corridor, in the 1936 three-tone pattern with a blue Pomeranian griffon emblem on the hull side.

**Below:** LTM 35 of Hptm. Mecke, commander of 2./Pz.Rgt.11, 1.leichte Division; finished in overall grey with the crosses, air identification panel and vehicle number in white.

**Below:** LTM 38, of the Pz.Abt.67, 3.leichte Division, with austere white markings.

vehicles to take advantage of natural cover was nearly as effective as sophisticated net camouflage in preventing air observation.

## National Insignia

The cross has been a traditional national emblem of the German and Austo-Hungarian states. This stems from its use by the Teutonic Knights and other Germanic orders between the thirteenth and fifteenth centuries who emblazoned their armour with the cross in their efforts to provide a religious pretext for their violent ventures into Eastern Europe. During the Great War, the Maltese and, later, the Greek cross ('balkan-kreuz') were used by the Central Powers. The Luftwaffe adopted the 'balkankreuz' in the 1930s. Initially, German tanks carried no national identification. In anticipation of the war, in August 1939 the Wehrmacht began painting its tanks with white 'balkankreuz'. The size of this insignia varied from unit to unit but it was generally of stubby proportions as compared to later versions. The crosses were carried prominently in eight locations: the front, rear and sides of the turret, and the front, rear and sides of the superstructure. The Wehrmacht obviously thought little of Polish anti-tank

gunners, as the white crosses on the sides and front of the tank ruined what little camouflage value the dark grey paint offered, and made excellent aiming points for Polish gun sights. After the first few days of fighting in September 1939, the German tankers learned their lesson and began subduing or removing the prominent frontal crosses. The earliest verifiable instance of this is shown in the photograph here of a Pz.Kpfw.I and a Pz.Kpfw.II of 5.Panzer Division knocked out at Pszczyna with their crosses overpainted in the centre in yellow. Although the photograph is dated 5 September, these tanks were more likely disabled on 2 September, when a small rearguard of the Polish 6th Infantry Division knocked out a score of tanks before 5.Panzer Division overran the town. This would seem to imply that the crosses may have been overpainted in yellow to reduce their visibility even before the outbreak of the war, or on the evening of 1 September at the latest. Other units completely obliterated their frontal crosses with grey paint, mud, grease or whatever else was handy. Some units did not change the insignia at all. It should be noted that, as a general rule, the national insignia was applied only on armoured vehicles and not on other vehicles of the Wehrmacht.

**Above:** An Sd.Kfz.22 advances alongside a column of captured Polish pontoon bridges through a field full of Polish prisoners of war. The armoured car has the usual white cross insignia, as well as a small white swallow insignia. The identification of the unit using the swallow sign is not known. (E.C.P.A., Paris)

**Right:** A knocked-out gepanzerter Kraftwagen (Fu) (Kfz.67a) displays a 'balkankreuz' insignia with the centre painted-out in grey. The paint on the front of the vehicle has peeled away under the heat of an engine fire. (George Balin)

# THE POLISH CAMPAIGN

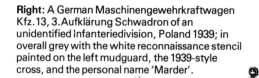

**Right:** A German Maschinengewehrkraftwagen Kfz.13, 3.Aufklärung Schwadron of an unidentified Infanteriedivision, Poland 1939; in overall grey with the white reconnaissance stencil painted on the left mudguard, the 1939-style cross, and the personal name 'Marder'.

**Below:** A Polish samochód pancerny wz.29, of 11dp, Mazowska Brygada Kawaleria in the standard three-tone pattern.

**Below:** A Polish czołg lekkich 7TPjw, of 2.batalion czołgów lekkich, 3.kompania in the standard 1936 pattern at the time of the occupation of Cieszyn, 1938. This tank carries the battalion's white cougar insignia. The stripe under the company marking and the extra radio equipment, denote that this is the company commander's tank.

**Below:** Polizei-Panzerkampfwagen ADGZ, of SS Heimwehr Danzig, Battle of the Gdansk Post Office in Danzig on 1 September 1939; in overall grey with runic SS letters and the death's head marking common to the SS. These insignia were repeated on the hull front.

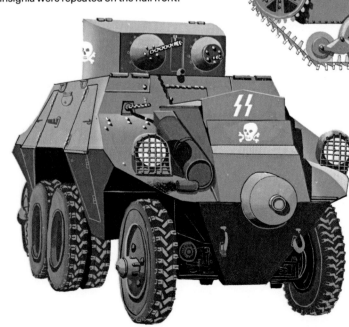

*Poland*: 1. batalion czołgów lekkich (1st Tank Battalion)

*Poland*: 2.batalion czołgów lekkich (2nd Tank Battalion)

*Poland*: 81.dywizjon pancerny (81st Armoured Troop)

*Poland*: 10 Brygada Kawaleria (10th Cavalry Brigade-B echelon)

*Poland*: Armoured train insignia

*Poland*: Pre-1936 national insignia on armoured cars

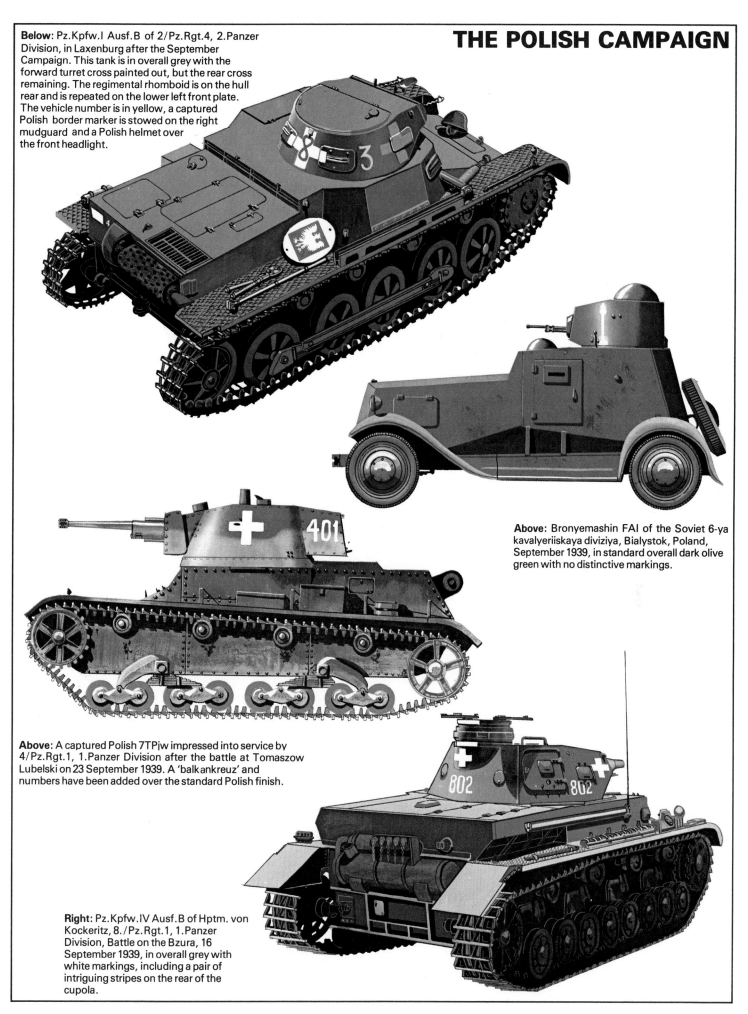

**Below:** Pz.Kpfw.I Ausf.B of 2/Pz.Rgt.4, 2.Panzer Division, in Laxenburg after the September Campaign. This tank is in overall grey with the forward turret cross painted out, but the rear cross remaining. The regimental rhomboid is on the hull rear and is repeated on the lower left front plate. The vehicle number is in yellow, a captured Polish border marker is stowed on the right mudguard and a Polish helmet over the front headlight.

**Above:** Bronyemashin FAI of the Soviet 6-ya kavalyeriiskaya diviziya, Bialystok, Poland, September 1939, in standard overall dark olive green with no distinctive markings.

**Above:** A captured Polish 7TPjw impressed into service by 4/Pz.Rgt.1, 1.Panzer Division after the battle at Tomaszow Lubelski on 23 September 1939. A 'balkankreuz' and numbers have been added over the standard Polish finish.

**Right:** Pz.Kpfw.IV Ausf.B of Hptm. von Kockeritz, 8./Pz.Rgt.1, 1.Panzer Division, Battle on the Bzura, 16 September 1939, in overall grey with white markings, including a pair of intriguing stripes on the rear of the cupola.

**Left:** A schwere Panzerfunk-wagen (Sd.Kfz.232) crosses a small irrigation ditch. No unit insignia is evident, and the crosses are carried in the usual location. (National Archives, Washington, DC)

**Below:** A column of 3.kompanie, Pz.Abt.67, of the 3.Leichte Division advances into Poland. The tanks are for the most part Pz.Kpfw. 38(t) Ausf.A (known as LTM 38 at the time), except for the second vehicle which is the rarely seen Pz.Kpfw.II Ausf.D. The markings consist of the typical 'balkankreuz' in white, and a small rhomboidal plate with the vehicle number painted on it; in the case of the lead vehicle '313'. (E.C.P.A., Paris)

As a result of their sobering experience in Poland in 1939, the Wehrmacht ordered the adoption of a modified 'balkankreuz' similar to that used by the Luftwaffe. The style adopted by the Luftwaffe consisted of a black cross outlined in white with a very thin black border. The Wehrmacht style usually consisted of the white outline only, though sometimes the black cross and border were added. New machines generally had just the white style.

## Air Identification

Air identification markings were commonly painted on the upper surfaces of armoured vehicles to help cooperation aeroplanes determine the extent of advance, coordinate artillery support and prevent accidental attacks by allied aircraft. It is difficult to determine with certainty what symbols were being used, owing to the lack of detailed written records in the archives or photographs which adequately show the upper surfaces of armoured vehicles. Certainly, the Wehrmacht began to use a large, white, painted rectangle as a means of air identification during the September Campaign, but it is not clear how widespread this practice was. This sign was carried on the engine deck, and was 1 by 0.5 metres in size. It was often supplemented by a white cross or swastika on the forward turret roof. By the time of the French Campaign in 1940, this symbol was in widespread use on most armoured vehicles. Interestingly enough, the supplementary roof cross was usually in the 1939 style even

during the French Campaign. On the Hanomag Sd.Kfz.251, the rectangle was sometimes carried on the front engine deck or, on other occasions, over the upper portion of the two rear doors. The white rectangle was not entirely successful as a means of air identification. Its light colour quickly became covered by dirt and grime, and it was easily obscured from the view of aerial observers by the glint of the sun off the rear deck or by personal stores carried on the back. Panzer crews soon found that the bright red, white and black Nazi flag made an ideal identification sign, and its use became widespread as the war went on. There were British Intelligence reports that some German armoured cars used yellow or red squares for air identification in 1940.

## Divisional Insignia

Though small and not overly prominent, the divisional signs of the Wehrmacht are especially interesting. For many years, this subject has been clouded by a good deal of contradictory and inaccurate material and, until the advent of Bruce Culver's book *Panzer Colours 2*, few 1940 signs were shown correctly. The trouble stemmed from the fact that many writers either relied too heavily on inaccurate wartime Intelligence reports, or did not realize that when some divisions adopted new insignia, their old signs passed to other units. The following descriptions of division insignia are based mainly on the large collection of German PK photographs in the National Archives, Washington DC, unique among the several large German wartime

**Above:** Pz.Kpfw.IV.B of 2/Pz.Rgt.4, 2.Panzer Division. The front hull cross has been totally obliterated, while the one on the turret is only partly obscured.

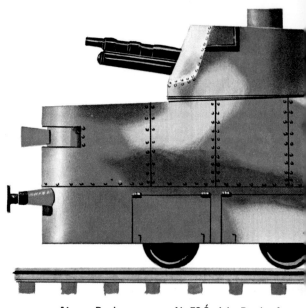

**Above:** Pociąg pancerny Nr.53 Śmiały, Battle of Mokra, 1 September 1939, in the official Polish 1936 pattern and colours.

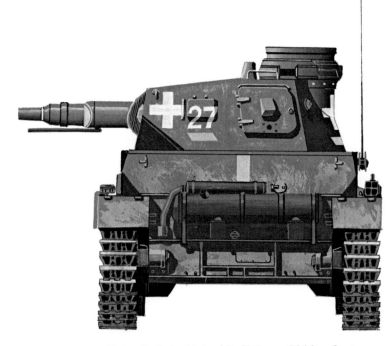

**Above:** Pz.Kpfw.IV. Ausf.B of 5.Panzer Division, Opatow, Poland. This view shows the vertical rear hull stripe and yellow turret rhomboid insignia peculiar to this division.

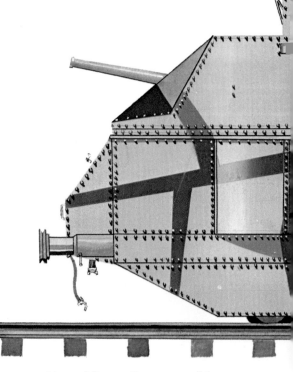

**Above:** A German Panzerzuge, of the 1.Eis.Pi.Ers.Btl.4/25, Poland, September 1939, in an unusual three-tone disruptive pattern with death's head insignias on the side and turret front.

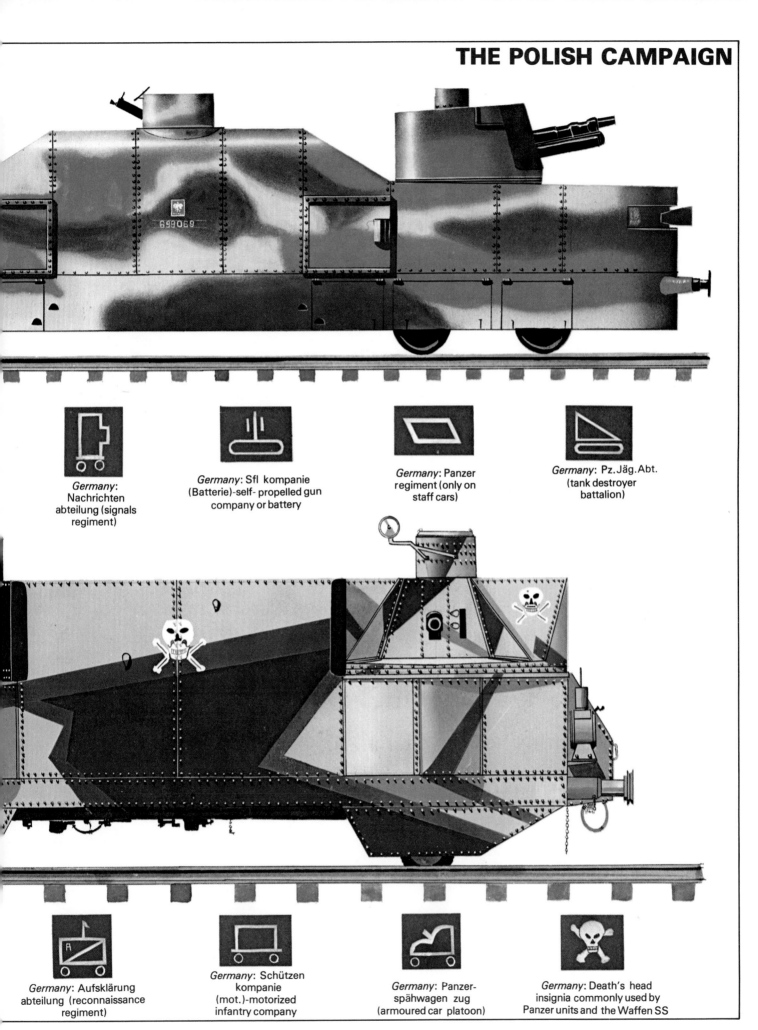

**Germany:**
Nachrichten
abteilung (signals
regiment)

**Germany:** Sfl kompanie
(Batterie)-self- propelled gun
company or battery

**Germany:** Panzer
regiment (only on
staff cars)

**Germany:** Pz.Jäg.Abt.
(tank destroyer
battalion)

**Germany:** Aufsklärung
abteilung (reconnaissance
regiment)

**Germany:** Schützen
kompanie
(mot.)-motorized
infantry company

**Germany:** Panzer-
spähwagen zug
(armoured car platoon)

**Germany:** Death's head
insignia commonly used by
Panzer units and the Waffen SS

**Opposite page, top:** A column of tanks of 4.Panzer Division advance on a hamlet during their attacks on the Wielkopolska Cavalry Brigade near Sochaczew in the third week of the war. The 4.Panzer Division fought a bitter two-day battle with the Wolynska Cavalry Brigade at the opening of the war before pushing on to attack Warsaw. Later in the campaign, the Division divided its attention between trying to break into Warsaw and trying to fight off attempts by Polish units, as here, to break in and reinforce the city. The Pz.Kpfw.I Ausf.A shown here belongs to the Aufklärung Zug of the HQ of 1.Abteilung, as is evident from the turret code (105) painted in yellow on both sides of the turret. The cross is barely evident at the rear, but is yellow with white edging. (National Archives, Washington, DC)

**Opposite page, bottom:** A schwere Panzerfunkwagen (Sd.Kfz.232), probably of 4.Panzer Division, advances down a street in the suburbs of Warsaw. The white 'balkankreuz' insignia is very evident on the radiator grill. (National Archives, Washington, DC)

**Top:** Three Pz.Kpfw.I Ausf.B of 4.Panzer Division try to break into Warsaw past a group of tramcars blockading a street in the Ochota section of the city. The crosses have been subdued with mud or dirt, but from the turret numbers (103, 112, 113) it is evident that these tanks belong to 1.kompanie. (National Archives, Washington, DC)

**Middle:** A Pz.Kpfw.IV Ausf.B and a klein Panzer Befehlswagen are drawn up for repairs in the market square of Opatow during the second week of the war. These vehicles belong to 5.Panzer Division. The turret of the Pz.Kpfw.IV is covered with dirt, but the yellow rhomboid insignia typical of 5.Panzer Division is visible under the white number 22. The 'balkankreuz' is also in white. (National Archives, Washington, DC)

**Bottom:** The market square in Opatow is full of vehicles of a heavy tank company of 5.Panzer Division. The Pz.Kpfw.IV in the left of the photograph shows the yellow rhomboid insignia below the rear turret cross, and a yellow band on the hull rear. (National Archives, Washington, DC)

# THE POLISH CAMPAIGN

*Germany*: 1. Panzer Division

*Germany*: 2. Panzer Division

*Germany*: 2. Panzer Division, Pz.Rgt.4

*Germany*: 3. Panzer Division

**Left:** Pz.Kpfw.II Ausf.B of 1.kompanie, 4.Panzer Division, carrying the subdued yellow crosses and three-pronged divisional star insignia.

# THE SCANDINAVIAN CAMPAIGN

*Germany*: 4. Panzer Division (1939)

*Germany*: 4. Panzer Division (1940)

*Germany*: 5. Panzer Division

*Germany*: 5. Panzer Division

*Germany*: 6. Panzer Division

*Germany*: 7. Panzer Division

**Left:** Pz.Kpfw.I Ausf.B of 1.kompanie, Pz.Abt.z.b.V.40, Copenhagen, Denmark, April 1940, with red and white turret numbers and the encircled 'V' regimental insignia in yellow. This insignia is repeated on the left hull rear and right hull superstructure front.

**Left:** Neubaufahrzeug of Pz.Abt.z.b.V.40, Oslo, Norway in April 1940 carrying the white elephant's head insignia peculiar to the three tanks of this type used in Scandinavia.

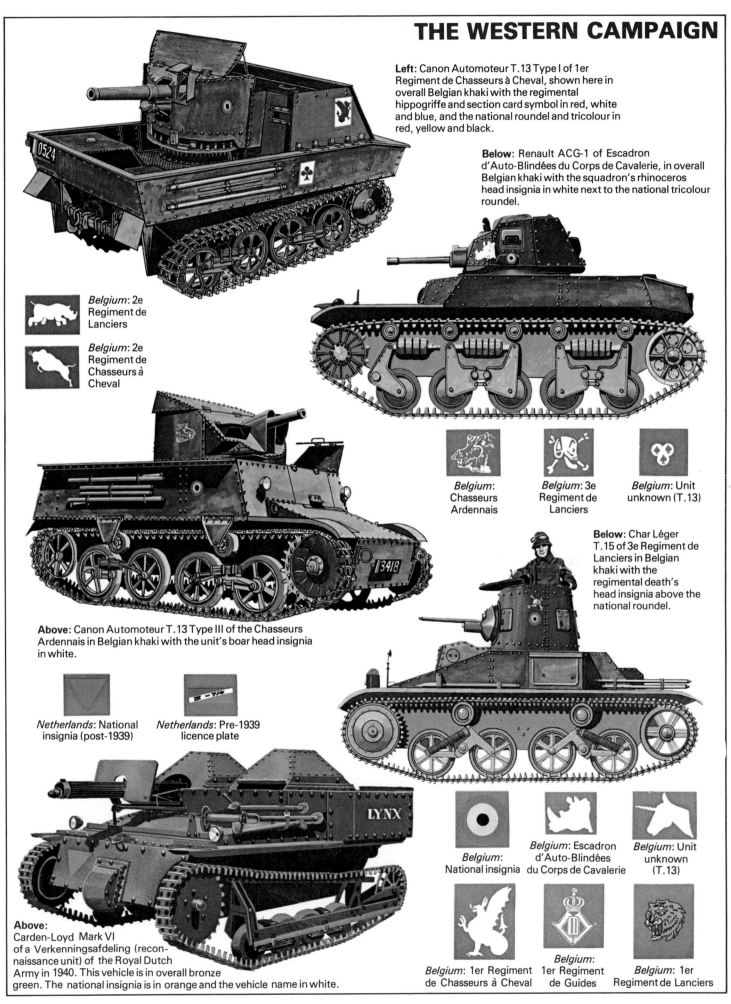

# THE WESTERN CAMPAIGN

**Left:** Canon Automoteur T.13 Type I of 1er Regiment de Chasseurs à Cheval, shown here in overall Belgian khaki with the regimental hippogriffe and section card symbol in red, white and blue, and the national roundel and tricolour in red, yellow and black.

**Below:** Renault ACG-1 of Escadron d'Auto-Blindées du Corps de Cavalerie, in overall Belgian khaki with the squadron's rhinoceros head insignia in white next to the national tricolour roundel.

*Belgium*: 2e Regiment de Lanciers

*Belgium*: 2e Regiment de Chasseurs à Cheval

*Belgium*: Chasseurs Ardennais

*Belgium*: 3e Regiment de Lanciers

*Belgium*: Unit unknown (T.13)

**Above:** Canon Automoteur T.13 Type III of the Chasseurs Ardennais in Belgian khaki with the unit's boar head insignia in white.

*Netherlands*: National insignia (post-1939)

*Netherlands*: Pre-1939 licence plate

**Below:** Char Léger T.15 of 3e Regiment de Lanciers in Belgian khaki with the regimental death's head insignia above the national roundel.

**Above:** Carden-Loyd Mark VI of a Verkenningsafdeling (reconnaissance unit) of the Royal Dutch Army in 1940. This vehicle is in overall bronze green. The national insignia is in orange and the vehicle name in white.

*Belgium*: National insignia

*Belgium*: Escadron d'Auto-Blindées du Corps de Cavalerie

*Belgium*: Unit unknown (T.13)

*Belgium*: 1er Regiment de Chasseurs à Cheval

*Belgium*: 1er Regiment de Guides

*Belgium*: 1er Regiment de Lanciers

collections in that it has the original captions, which frequently identify units shown in the photographs.

The insignia of the Panzer divisions were usually carried in several places on the hull superstructure, and generally were painted in white or yellow.

### 1.Panzer Division

From photographic evidence, the 1.Pz.Div. did not use a divisional insignia on its tanks during the September Campaign of 1939. In 1940, the division used a white oakleaf emblem which, in contrast to most other units, was often carried on the turret. The 1.Panzer Division displayed other idiosyncracies in its markings. Several photographs of the unit's Pz.Kpfw.IIIs and Pz.Kpfw.IVs show the use of small geometric symbols, such as triangles, bands and squares behind the turret cupola. Apparently, tanks of Pz.Rgt.1 were distinguished from those of Pz.Rgt.2 by underlining the turret numbers on Pz.Rgt.2 with a white band.

### 2.Panzer Division

From the handful of photographs available of tanks from the 2.Pz.Div. in Poland in 1939, it is not clear whether the divisional emblem, two small yellow dots, was used in the September Campaign, although it was standard during the Battle of France. One peculiarity of the 2.Pz.Div. was the use of a painted white rhomboid insignia instead of the removable, black, tactical number plates used in other divisions. This insignia was usually carried on the front and rear of the hull and occasionally on the turret sides. The regimental number usually came next, followed by the divisional insignia which, when used, appeared below it. One inexplicable marking used in 1939 was the imposition of a red '8' over the rear turret cross. The 2.Panzer Division may have used playing card symbols for markings in 1940.

### 3.Panzer Division

Lacking verifiable photographs of 3.Panzer Division in Poland, it is not known if its divisional insignia, a lop-sided 'E', was used in 1939. It was in common use by 1940, but was so small that it is often difficult to spot on photographs.

### 4.Panzer Division

During the Polish Campaign, 4.Panzer Division appears to have used a three-pronged star in yellow or white. By the time of the Battle of France, this had been replaced by the official circular 'man-rune' emblem. In 1940, Panzer Regiment 36 was distinguished from Panzer Regiment 35 by the use of a small, white dot after the turret numbers.

### 5.Panzer Division

While 5.Pz.Div. did not use a divisional insignia in 1939, its tanks carried distinctive markings. A white or yellow elongated rhomboid, sometimes bisected by a black band, was carried on the lower sides and rear of the turret. The difference between the plain and bisected rhomboid may have been used to distinguish tanks of Panzer Regiment 15 from those of Panzer Regiment 31. Some of the division's tanks also had a vertical band painted on the hull rear. During the Battle of France, the divisional insignia was usually a yellow inverted 'Y' with a single dot at its base. However, some dated photographs would indicate that the later yellow 'X' insignia was also used.

### 1-4.Leichte Divisionen

The Leichte Divisionen (light divisions) which served in 1939 in Poland were motorized cavalry divisions comparable to the French DLM's (Division Légère Mécanique). They did not perform well in the September Campaign and were reorganized into Panzer divisions in time for the Battle of France. No distinctive divisional emblems are known from photographs.

### 6.Panzer Division

The 6.Panzer Division was formerly 1.Leichte Division. In France in 1940, it used an inverted 'Y' with two dots. This unit was unusual in that few of its tanks had the large turret numbers common to the vehicles of most other divisions.

### 7.Panzer Division

Formerly the 2.Leichte Division, 7.Panzer Division came under the command of Erwin Rommel in the

**Below:** A leichte Panzerfunk-wagen (Sd.Kfz.223) and a leichte Panzerspähwagen (Sd.Kfz.221) guard a level crossing. The white 'balkankreuz' are prominently displayed. (E.C.P.A., Paris)

**Top:** A Pz.Kpfw.IV Ausf.B has a new track fitted while being repaired at Opatow. The tank has a yellow vertical band on the centre of the rear plate above the silencer, the purpose of which is not certain. (National Archives, Washington, DC)

**Middle:** A Pz.Kpfw.IV Ausf.B parades through the streets of Warsaw after the surrender of the city. The 'balkankreuz' marking is very evident on the hull front. While many units painted out such markings, in other units they remained untouched throughout the campaign. (National Archives, Washington, DC)

**Bottom:** A formation of Pz.Kpfw.II Ausf.B parade before Hitler's review stand in Warsaw on 5 October 1939. No markings are evident except for the cross insignia. (National Archives, Washington, DC)

# THE WESTERN CAMPAIGN

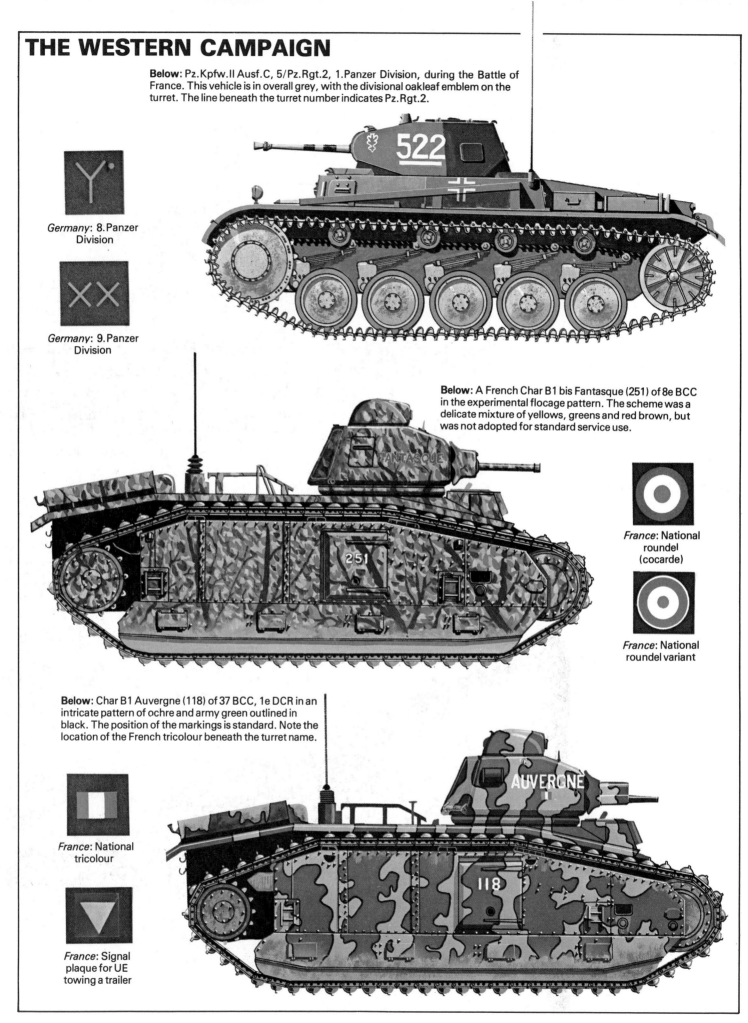

**Below:** Pz.Kpfw.II Ausf.C, 5/Pz.Rgt.2, 1.Panzer Division, during the Battle of France. This vehicle is in overall grey, with the divisional oakleaf emblem on the turret. The line beneath the turret number indicates Pz.Rgt.2.

*Germany*: 8.Panzer Division

*Germany*: 9.Panzer Division

**Below:** A French Char B1 bis Fantasque (251) of 8e BCC in the experimental flocage pattern. The scheme was a delicate mixture of yellows, greens and red brown, but was not adopted for standard service use.

*France*: National roundel (cocarde)

*France*: National roundel variant

**Below:** Char B1 Auvergne (118) of 37 BCC, 1e DCR in an intricate pattern of ochre and army green outlined in black. The position of the markings is standard. Note the location of the French tricolour beneath the turret name.

*France*: National tricolour

*France*: Signal plaque for UE towing a trailer

**Above:** A group of Pz.Kpfw.Is and IIs are shipped back to Germany in November, 1939. While the plain white cross has been left untouched on the leading vehicle, barely evident is the remains of a death's head insignia in front of this, painted out in grey.
(National Archives, Washington, DC)

**Right:** A pair of Panzerspäh-wagen (Sd.Kfz.263) during the Phoney War period. The last of the two still has the solid white 1939 cross, while the leading vehicle has had the centre of the white cross painted in grey, creating the newer 1940 style. The diagonally bisected rectangle sign of an Aufklärung abteilung (reconnaissance battalion) is barely evident on the left mud-guard of the first vehicle.
(National Archives, Washington, DC)

French Campaign. Its insignia was a yellow inverted 'Y' with three dots. The division's tanks were also distinguishable by their unusually large turret numbers, which often took the form of red numerals with thin white outlines. There have been suggestions that these numerals may have been painted in First World War infantry colours to distinguish between different regiments or battalions, but there is no hard evidence of this.

## 8. Panzer Division
Formerly the 3.Leichte Division, the markings of 8.Pz.Div. in France are not certain owing to a lack of good photographs. A yellow 'Y' with a single dot has been attributed to the division, but the matter is still open.

## 9. Panzer Division
Formerly 4.Leichte Division, 9.Panzer Division used a pair of yellow 'X's during the campaign in the Low Countries and France. This marking has caused some confusion as it was later adopted by 6.Panzer Division in 1941.

## 10. Panzer Division
This division was not completely formed in 1939 but elements of it fought as Panzer Verband Ostpreussen. Its two regiments, Panzer Regiment 8 and Panzer Regiment 9, each had individual insignia, a white 'wolfsangel' and a reverse stencil bison respectively. Whether these were used in Poland is not known. In France, the regimental insignia was used in addition to the divisional insignia, which was a yellow 'Y' with three dots or strokes.

## Panzer Division Kempf
Nothing is known of the markings of this unit which served in Poland.

## Special Battalion Insignia
It was not common German practice to allow the use of heraldic insignia by units below divisional level but, nonetheless, this did occur.

## Pz.Abt.z.B.v. 40
Pz.Abt.z.B.v.40 was a special support unit formed for the invasion of Scandinavia. Its three companies went to Norway and one later went to Denmark. The standard marking was a yellow, circled 'V' with the company number in the lower right quadrant, but there were several exceptions. Three Neubaufahrzeuge (experimental medium tanks with three turrets) were sent with the unit to Oslo, where they were widely photographed for propaganda purposes. These machines had an elephant's head insignia painted on the left of the glacis plate. Photographs purporting to show Pz.Kpfw.IIIs in Norway in 1940 show a small, white, rectangular insignia with a hollow, grey triangle within.

## Panzer Jäger Abteilung
There were five Panzer Jäger Abteilung in service in 1940 equipped with the 4.7cm PAK(t) Sf: Pz.Jäg.Abt. 521, 605, 616, 643 and 650. Pz.Jäg. Abt. 643 used a white, Maltese cross insignia on the superstructure sides and hull rear. Pz.Jäg.Abt. 521 shown in the photograph right, used a stylized elk's head and shield emblem. The other three battalions used no distinctive insignia, judging from photographs.

## Schwere Infanterie Geschütz Kompanie
There were six heavy infantry support companies in service in 1940 equipped with the sIG33 Sf. These companies were ostensibly independent but functionally

were attached to the Panzer divisions. None of these companies had their own insignia, though s.Inf.Ges.Kp. 702 used that of 1.Panzer Division with which it served. More often, the company carried its number on the superstructure front. It was common practice to name vehicles with nicknames derived from the battery letter: B-Bismarck, E-Edith, for example. The battery letter was usually carried on the sides of the superstructure on the oval cover plate over the howitzer's wheel hub, while the name was generally in the centre of the front superstructure.

## Tactical Insignia
### Unit signs
Aside from the heraldic divisional and regimental insignia, German vehicles were generally marked with small geometric signs to more precisely identify their attachment within a division or regiment. These signs were derived from the symbols used on combat maps— outlined in the 1936 book *Oertzenscher Taschenkalender* f.d. Offz.d.H.Berlin—and in subsequent booklets, and were usually painted in white or yellow on the left front and right rear of the vehicle.

Left: A column passes a Mann-schaftstransportwagen (troop transporter) Sd.Kfz.251 of 10.kompanie, Schützen Brigade 1 of 1.Panzer Division shortly after the division crossed the Maas River near Floing on 13 May 1940. The vehicle on the right has the upper part of the rear doors painted white as an air identification marking. Below this is the divisional oakleaf sign, and the stencilled sign for a motorized infantry (Schützen) company, followed by the company number (10). The Wehrmacht Heer (Armed Forces Army) licence plate is also clearly visible. A StuG Sd.Kfz.142 can be seen farther down the road. (National Archives, Washington, DC)

Below: Tanks of HQ of 2.kompanie, Pz.Rgt.2 of 1.Panzer Division stop to rest in a small town in Belgium on 12 May 1940. The Pz.Kpfw.IIs have the divisional oakleaf emblem carried on the turret rear, with the vehicle number below it. (National Archives, Washington, DC)

These insignia were not used on tanks ordinarily, for reasons explained below, but were carried on other armoured vehicles, such as armoured cars in Aufklärung Abteilung (reconnaissance battalions) or Nachrichtung kompanie (signals companies), on armoured self-propelled guns of the Panzer Jäger Abteilung (tank destroyer battalions) and schwere Infanterie Geschütz Kompanie (heavy infantry support gun companies), or on the armoured half-tracks of Schützen (motorized infantry) units.

There were hundreds of these insignia for everything down to wheeled field kitchens. Few were applied to armoured vehicles, and as they have been covered adequately elsewhere, they will not be covered here. The symbols were from 8 to 20cm high depending on the type, and 14 to 20cm wide. They could be qualified by the addition of a number or a symbol to designate the unit more precisely; for example, a '4' after the wheeled rectangle of a motorized infantry platoon would indicate Infanteriezug 4.

In place of these painted symbols, tanks serving in the Panzer regiments used a thin metal plate, cut in the shape for a tank used in maps (rhomboid). There were usually three of these plates, to be carried on both sides

Right: A Pz.Kpfw.I Ausf.B and
two Pz.Kpfw.IV Ausf.B of
Pz.Rgt.1, 1.Panzer Division
halt on the outskirts of Bertrix,
Belgium on 12 May 1940. On the
rear of the Pz.Kpfw.I's turret is
the divisional oakleaf sign. The
turret number '623' indicates that
it is the third vehicle of 2.zug,
6.kompanie. The other two tanks
belong to 8.kompanie, Pz.Rgt.1.
(National Archives, Washington,
DC)

Below: This Panzer Befehlswagen
of 2/Pz.Rgt.2, 1.Panzer Division
slid into a bomb crater on 12 May
1940 during the Belgian
Campaign. It displays a standard
assortment of markings,
including a white recognition
rectangle on the engine deck, a
solid white air recognition cross
on the turret roof, turret numbers
'II01' (indicating HQ of
2.Abteilung) with a bar underlining them, indicating Pz.Rgt.2.
(National Archives, Washington,
DC)

and at the rear, and they were painted black. Each tank would have its individual number painted on the plate. These plates were removable for security purposes, though by the time of the Battle of France in 1940 they had become largely superfluous owing to the use of large turret numbers bearing the same information, and they gradually disappeared from use after 1940.

The use of turret numbers and the small numbers on the plates followed the same general rules. The first of the three numbers indicated kompanie (company), the second, zug (platoon) and the third was the individual vehicle number. Hence, '124' would be the fourth tank

of the second platoon of the first company. At the time, German tank platoons numbered from four to five tanks per platoon and four platoons per company. The tanks of the company's headquarters section would generally be numbered 101, 102; 201, 202, etc. though on occasion the sequence for the two vehicles would be 100, 101; 200, 201, etc. The tanks of the headquarters of the Abteilung (battalion) would be prefaced by the roman numeral 'I'. As there were two battalions per regiment, the first battalion would be prefaced with 'I' and the second with 'II'. Therefore, the vehicles were numbered as I01, I02; II01, II02. This pattern was not

**Top:** A column of Pz.Kpfw.IIIs of Pz.Rgt.1, 1.Panzer Division on the road near Bouillon, Luxembourg on 13 May 1940, immediately before the drive on Sedan across the French border. On the last vehicle can be seen a curious triangular marking behind the cupola, and on the vehicle in front a vertical bar is evident. The meaning of these insignia is not known. (National Archives, Washington, DC)

**Middle:** Only 10 of these monstrous 8.8cm Flak 18 (Sfl) auf Zugkraftwagen 12t were produced, and they served with 8.schwere Pz.Jäg.Abt. in Poland and France. There were no battalion markings, only the national insignia and the von Kleist corps letter on the right mudguard. (E.C.P.A., Paris)

**Bottom:** An ambulance improvized on a Pz.Kpfw.I Ausf.B chassis from Pz.Rgt.1 of 1.Panzer Division, rests by the roadside after being gutted by a mine. The vehicle is prominently marked with the white cross insignia, and carries the number '18' on the lower bow plate. Several units used light tanks for battlefield recovery of wounded tankers under fire. (National Archives, Washington, DC)

**Opposite page, top:** A Pz.Kpfw.III Ausf.F of 2/Rgt.1, 1.Panzer Division advances on Bouillon on 13 May 1940. No divisional insignia is evident. Judging from the amount of stores carried on the rear deck, it is not surprising that the Wehrmacht dropped the white recognition rectangle in favour of a more conspicuous Nazi flag. (National Archives, Washington, DC)

**Opposite page bottom:** A Pz.Kpfw.II Ausf.B of 4.kompanie, Pz.Rgt.1, 1.Panzer Division, crosses the Maas River on 14 May 1940. The white, painted air recognition rectangle can be seen overlapping the edge of the engine deck, almost concealed beneath the more useful swastika flag. (National Archives, Washington, DC)

**Left:** A Pz.Kpfw.II Ausf.b moves forward in support of an infantry unit. On the left corner of the hull superstructure is the insignia of 3.Panzer Division. (National Archives, Washington, DC)

**Below:** A leichte Panzerspähwagen (Sd.Kfz.221) of Aufklärung Abteilung 7, 4.Panzer Division near Chateau-Thierry, June 1940. No markings are evident except for the small stencilled sign of 1.kompanie of an Aufklärung Abteilung on the left mudguard. (National Archives, Washington, DC)

universally followed, and some regiments used A and B for the two battalions instead: for example A01, B01, etc. The usual sequence for these numbers was -01 (battalion commander), -02 (executive officer), -03 (signals officer), -04 (ordnance officer). Further numbers in the sequence were usually those of the battalion reconnaissance platoon. The tanks of regimental headquarters used the same system, but used the prefix 'R', as in R01, R02, etc. There were several variations on this; in some regiments the code 'RN' was used, as in RN1 (Regiment Nachrichten-Regimental Transmissions); also, the prefix 'RL' was seen (Regiment Leichte). Perhaps the rarest prefix was 'F' (Film) which was used on a handful of Pz.Kpfw.1s assigned to divisional film teams.

*Licence plates*
While not carried on fully tracked armoured vehicles, wheeled and half-tracked armoured vehicles carried the same type of licence plate issued to unarmoured transport. One or, occasionally, two plates were carried on the rear mudguard. These plates were 20cm high by 32cm wide and had the upper corners clipped. They were made of thin metal, painted white with black borders and black numerals. There was a practice of stamping the plates with a field post office number in the form of a small red circular design with the Wehrmacht eagle in the centre, but this habit was not widespread in France in 1940. On most armoured vehicles, the licence number on the front was painted directly on the armour. This took the form of a thin

**Right:** A column of Pz.Kpfw.IV Ausf.C and Ausf.D display the insignia of 2.Panzer Division. The divisional insignia, two small dots, can be seen beneath the yellow rhomboid insignia on the left bow front and left-hand corner of the super-structure. The rhomboid is followed by the company number (5). No turret numbers are evident. (E.C.P.A., Paris)

**Below:** A Pz.Kpfw.IV Ausf.D of Pz.Rgt.9, 10.Panzer Division taking target practice during training on 2 April 1940. The subdued regimental bison insignia can be seen on the forward side of the turret. (National Archives, Washington, DC)

**Left:** Hptm.Jesse, commander of the Pz.Rgt.36 of 4.Panzer Division, watches his unit advance from the vantage of his grosse Panzer Befehlswagen (gr.Pz.Bef.Wg.) 17 May 1940. Under the bundle of sticks can be seen the edge of the white rectangular air recognition sign painted on the engine deck and supplanted by the Nazi flag tied between the radio aerial. On the turret rear can be seen the code 'RN1' (Regiment Nachrichtung-1) and the small dot indicating Pz.Rgt.36. (National Archives, Washington, DC)

**Below:** A rain-soaked schwere Panzerfunkwagen (Sd.Kfz.232) of 3.Panzer Division advances near the Marne crossing outside Chateau-Thierry on 12 June 1940. The divisional insignia can be seen on the right-hand corner of the hull front. On the bow itself are the scrapped remains of a solid white 1939-style 'balkankreuz' marking. This vehicle flies a small Nazi pennant over the left mudguard. (National Archives, Washington, DC)

**Top:** A Pz.Kpfw.II leads a column from Pz.Rgt.36, 4.Panzer Division into Englefontaine on 21 May 1940. The circular yellow man-rune insignia is plainly visible on the superstructure front. (National Archives, Washington, DC)

**Middle:** A schwere Panzerfunkwagen (Sd.Kfz.263) crosses a pontoon bridge over the Marne River near Chateau-Thierry on 12 June 1940. Above the licence plate on the left can be seen the circular 4.Panzer Division insignia. On the engine deck, a large white rectangular insignia is evident behind the bicycle. (National Archives, Washington, DC)

**Bottom:** Several divisions were assigned Propaganda Kompanie photographers. This film crew was assigned its own tank, a Pz.Kpfw.1 Ausf.A, and was attached to Pz.Rgt.36, 4.Panzer Division. The turret code is a unique '1F', which indicates first vehicle, Film, Pz. Rgt.36. A white air recognition rectangle can be seen on the rear deck near the cloth sack. (National Archives, Washington, DC)

**Left:** A Munitionsschlepper (ammunition carrier) of 3.Panzer Division sits astride a crossroads in Villenaux, France on 16 June 1940. Besides the lopsided 'E' divisional insignia, the vehicle has a white death's head insignia, which was a frequent decoration associated with Panzer units. (National Archives, Washington, DC)

**Below:** This Pz.Kpfw.I Ausf.B served with Aufklärung Zug, Stab, 2.Abteilung, Pz.Rgt.36, 4.Panzer Division. The turret code 'IIL5' indicates that 2.Abteilung was a light battalion. The turret letters and divisional insignia on the upper left corner of the hull rear were painted in yellow, while the cross is a plain white outline. Note that the turret lettering was repeated on both sides as well as the rear. (National Archives, Washington, DC)

**Above:** A pair of Pz.Kpfw.IV Ausf.D of Rommel's 7.Panzer Division training prior to the French Campaign. This division usually had very large turret numbers with the centres coloured in. The divisional insignia is evident on the upper left corner of the hull superstructure. (National Archives, Washington, DC)

rectangle, positioned centrally, 9cm high and 47.5cm long. The number itself was usually six digits prefixed by a branch of service code: WH (Wehrmacht), WL (Luftwaffe), SS (Waffen SS). The formation of the early Panzer and light divisions was controlled by four administrative motorized corps: the XIV, responsible for new formations; the XV, responsible for the first three light divisions; the XVI, responsible for the active Panzer divisions; and the XIX, formed in 1939. The first three of these corps were distributed blocks of numbers, which they added to the licence plates issued to vehicles of their divisions.

XIV Motorized Corps: 140000-149999; 240000-249999.

XV Motorized Corps: 150000-159999; 250000-259000.

XVI Motorized Corps: 160000-169999; 260000-269999.

**Miscellaneous Markings**

German tanks on leaving the factories often had their chassis numbers painted in small, white digits on the superstructure. These were usually overpainted on receipt by the regiment, but they were occasionally evident. Some typical chassis number blocks appropriate to vehicles of the 1939-40 campaigns were:

Pz.Kpfw.I: 9001-16500.

Pz.Kpfw.II: 20001-20075; 21001-21025; 21101-28000.

Pz.Kpfw.III: 60201-60215; 60301-60496; 61001-61650.

Pz.Kpfw.IV: 80101-80135; 80201-80245; 80301-80440; 80501-(post-campaign).

Another style of marking was the stowage or instruction label. A typical sample of this variety of marking was the small, white stencilled '3.5 atu' script carried on the mudguard above each of the wheels of the Sd.Kfz.232. This marking indicated the proper air pressure for the tyres, and varied depending upon the vehicle. The Wehrmacht frequently used an ordinary railroad loading stencil on tanks transported by rail, but this marking is not in evidence in many photographs from the 1939-40 campaigns.

A convoy-marking typical of rear echelon transport, but occasionally seen on combat vehicles, was the use of a white, L-shaped outline on the lower edges of the mudguard. This helped traffic controllers and neighbouring drivers determine the proximity of other vehicles, especially in poor visibility. Personal names were sometimes carried on German tanks, but certainly not as prevalently as on British or French tanks. Rank pennants were sometimes flown from staff armoured cars or half-tracks, but it was not common in combat.

One marking frequently seen during the French Campaign was the use of the letters 'K' and 'G' on the fronts of vehicles of Kleist's and Guderian's units. These markings became most common during the Fall Rot (Plan Red) phase when the Panzer divisions were shuffled around. Guderian controlled 1., 2., 6., and 8.Panzer Divisionen, and von Kleist controlled 3., 4., 9. and 10. Panzer Divisionen. There were a few anomalies in this system. For example, there are photographs of a staff car of 1.Panzer Division with a 'K', which may refer to the divisional commander (Kirschner) rather than von Kleist.

**Opposite page:** A Pz.IV Ausf.D of 1.Panzer Division displaying no evident divisional insignia, which were often absent from this division's tanks. Pz.Kpfw.IVs were generally assigned to the 4. and 8.kompanie of Panzer Abteilungen during the French Campaign. Therefore, their turret numbers usually began with '4' or '8'. (National Archives, Washington, DC)

**Opposite page, bottom:** A Pz.Kpfw.II and Pz.Kpfw.III show the insignia of 2.kompanie, Pz.Rgt.36, 4.Panzer Division. The dot after the turret numbers was used to distinguish Pz.Rgt.36 from Pz.Rgt.35, the other regiment of 4.Panzer Division. This style of marking was abandoned when the Panzer divisions were subsequently reorganized with only one regiment apiece. (National Archives, Washington, DC)

**Top:** This damaged Munitionsschlepper auf Fgst.Pz.Kpfw.I Ausf.A of 4.Panzer Division clearly shows the position of the white air identification rectangle on the engine deck. (National Archives, Washington, DC)

**Middle:** The 7.Panzer Division was one of two divisions to use the Pz.Kpfw.38(t) during the French Campaign. This photograph was taken during manoeuvres near Blévy on 22 November 1940, but shows markings typical of those used during the fighting. Note the characteristic large turret numbers. (National Archives, Washington, DC)

**Bottom:** A Mannschafts-transportwagen Sd.Kfz.251 Ausf.B on training manoeuvres in Germany, 2 April 1940. It belonged to 9.kompanie, Schützen Brigade 5, 5.Panzer Division. The stencilled insignia for a motorized infantry company is carried on the hull rear, and immediately below this, and barely evident, is a yellow 'X', one of the signs of 5.Panzer Division during 1940. (National Archives, Washington, DC)

**Top:** A column of Pz.Kpfw.IIIs of 5.kompanie, Pz.Rgt.7., 10.Panzer Division conduct exercises in the Suippes area after the Battle of France. Besides the regimental bison insignia, the divisional sign in yellow is evident near the rear cross. The Pz.Rgt.7 generally used only the company number on the turret. (National Archives, Washington, DC)

**Bottom:** This 15cm sIG (Sfl.) auf Fgst. Pz.Kpfw.I belonged to sIG Kp.706, 10.Panzer Division. The company number can be seen above the letter for von Kleist's corps. The battery letter 'E' is visible on the other side. A name in small lettering can barely be seen under the gun. These self-propelled gun companies seldom carried divisional insignia since they were supposed to be independent Heeres Truppen. (National Archives, Washington, DC)

**Right:** Panzerfunkwagen (Sd.Kfz.263) 8-rad, of Gen. Erwin Rommel, Division Stab, 7.Panzer Division, Battle of France. This vehicle carries the divisional insignia and the signals platoon insignia in yellow on the corner of the bow, and air pressure markings for the tyres in white on the mudguards. On the mudguard is the divisional pennant. The vehicle licence was WH-143149 and was painted in the usual place on the bow.

# THE WESTERN CAMPAIGN

**Below:** Char Moyen D2 Bouvines (2011) of 19e BCC, 4 DCR, in overall army green with ochre swatches outlined in black. The white circle and red diamond indicate 1st company, 3rd section. Besides the standard markings, the tank has the name Janet Lou painted on the right hull front. Note the dirty white circle on the hull front.

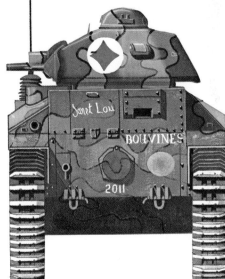

*Germany*: 10. Panzer Division

*Germany*: 10. Panzer Division (variation)

*Germany*: 10. Panzer Division, Pz.Rgt.9

**Below:** Sd.Kfz.222 of an unidentified unit, during the French Campaign. It is in overall grey with a prominent air identification panel painted over the rear engine deck and radiator vents outlined in white.

**Below:** Cruiser Tank Mk.III (A.13) of B Company headquarters, 3rd RTR, 1st Armoured Division in Calais painted in the G.3/G.4 scheme. The yellow company sign was carried on the front and side of the turret. On the bow from right to left are the yellow bridging circle with '14' in black, the green and white regimental code sign and the white divisional rhinoceros sign. On the right side of the turret front is the white mobilization number (0042) with the light green/blue/light green embarkation stripes below it.

*U.K.*: 1st Infantry Division

*U.K.*: 13th/18th Hussars (Army pennant)

*U.K.*: 13th/18th Hussars (regimental insignia)

| Wehrmacht tank inventory [1] | | |
| --- | --- | --- |
| Type | 1 September 1939 | 1 May 1940 |
| Pz.Kpfw. I | 1,445 | 1,077 |
| Pz.Kpfw. II | 1,223 | 1,092 |
| Pz.Kpfw. III (3.7cm) | 98 | 381 |
| Pz.Kpfw. IV | 211 | 290 |
| Command tanks | 215 | 244 |
| Pz.Kpfw. 35(t) (LTM 35) | 196 | 143 |
| Pz.Kpfw. 38(t) (LTM 38) | 78 | 238 |
| Light armoured cars [2] | 718 | 800 |
| Heavy armoured cars [3] | 307 | 333 |
| MTW Sd.Kfz. 251 [4] | 68 | 338 |
| 4.7cm PAK (Sf) | – | 100 |
| StuG III | 5 | 20 |
| 15cm sIG Sf | – | 38 |

1. Courtesy of Thomas L. Jentz. 2. Sd.Kfz.13, 14, 221, 222 and 223. 3. Sd.Kfz.231, 232 and 263. 4. Number produced to this date; no information available on inventory.

| Order of battle of German armoured units during the Polish Campaign, 1 September 1939 [1] | | |
| --- | --- | --- |
| Division | Unit | Tank strength |
| 1.Panzer Division | Pz.Rgt. 1 & 2 | 308 |
| 2.Panzer Division | Pz.Rgt. 3 & 4 | 323 |
| 3.Panzer Division | Pz.Rgt. 5 & 6, Pz.Lehr.Abt. | 394 |
| 4.Panzer Division | Pz.Rgt. 35 & 36 | 295 |
| 5.Panzer Division | Pz.Rgt. 15 & 31 | 323 |
| 10.Panzer Division | Pz.Rgt. 8 | 157 |
| Panzer Division Kempf | Pz.Rgt. 7 | 166 |
| 1.Leichte Division | Pz.Rgt. 11, Pz.Abt. 65 | 229 (with LTM 35 tanks) |
| 2.Leichte Division | Pz.Abt. (verlostet) 66 | 83 |
| 3.Leichte Division | Pz.Abt. 67 | 104 (with LTM 38 tanks) |
| 4.Leichte Division | Pz.Abt. (verlostet) 33 | 83 |
| Ind. Heeres Truppen | I.Abt./Pz.Rgt. 23 | 74 |
|  | I.Abt./Pz.Rgt. 25 | 74 |

(Total strength was 2,626 tanks out of 3,466 tanks and command tanks in the Wehrmacht inventory, 1 September 1939.)

| Abbreviation | German | English |
| --- | --- | --- |
| Aufkl. Abt. | Aufklärungs Abteilung | Reconnaissance battalion |
|  | Heeres Truppen | Army troops (non-divisional units attached to Army command) |
| Pio. Btl. | Pionere Batalion | Pioneer battalion |
| Pz. Jäg. Abt. | Panzer Jäger Abteilung | Self-propelled tank destroyer battalion |

| Abbreviation | German | English |
| --- | --- | --- |
| Schtz. Brig. | Schützen Brigade | Motorized infantry brigade |
| sfl | Selbstfahrlafette | Self-propelled |
| sIG Kp | schwere Infantrie Geschütz kompanie | Heavy infantry gun company |

| Division | Tank units | Tank strength | | Infantry units | Reconnaissance units | Engineer units |
|---|---|---|---|---|---|---|
| | | Light tanks and command tanks[2] | Gun-armed tanks[3] | | | |
| 1.Panzer Division | Pz.Rgt. 1 & 2 | 161 | 98 | Schtz.Brig. 1[6] sIG Kp. 702 | Aufkl.Abt. 4[4] | Pio.Btl. 37[5] |
| 2.Panzer Division | Pz.Rgt. 3 & 4 | 175 | 90 | Schtz.Brig. 2 sIG Kp. 703 | Aufkl.Abt. 5 | Pio.Btl. 38 |
| 3.Panzer Division | Pz.Rgt. 5 & 6 | 273 | 68 | Schtz.Brig. 3 | Aufkl.Abt. 3 | Pio.Btl. 39 |
| 4.Panzer Division | Pz.Rgt. 35 & 36 | 259 | 64 | Schtz.Brig. 4 | Aufkl.Abt. 7 | Pio.Btl. 79 |
| 5.Panzer Division | Pz.Rgt. 15 & 31 | 243 | 84 | Schtz.Brig. 5 sIG Kp. 704 | Aufkl.Abt. 8 | Pio.Btl. 89 |
| 6.Panzer Division | Pz.Rgt. 11, Pz.Abt. 65 | 59 | 159 | Schtz.Brig. 6 | Aufkl.Abt. 57 | Pio.Btl. 57 |
| 7.Panzer Division | Pz.Rgt. 25 | 109 | 110 | Schtz.Brig. 7 sIG Kp. 705 | Aufkl.Abt. 37 | Pio.Btl. 58 |
| 8.Panzer Division | Pz.Rgt. 10 | 58 | 154 | Schtz.Brig. 8 | Aufkl.Abt. 59 | Pio.Btl. 59 |
| 9.Panzer Division | Pz.Rgt. 33 | 97 | 56 | Schtz.Brig. 9 sIG Kp. 701 | Aufkl.Rgt. 9 | Pio.Btl. 86 |
| 10.Panzer Division | Pz.Rgt. 7 & 8 | 185 | 90 | Schtz.Brig. 10 sIG Kp. 706 | Aufkl.Abt. 90 | Pio.Btl. 49 |

Order of battle of German armoured units during Battle of France, 10 May 1940[1]

| Independent Heeres Truppen | 4.7cm Pak(t) Sfl | StuG III |
|---|---|---|
| Heeres Pz.Jäg.Abt.(Sfl) 521 | 18 | |
| Heeres Pz.Jäg.Abt.(Sfl) 605 | 18 | |
| Heeres Pz.Jäg.Abt.(Sfl) 616 | 27 | |
| Heeres Pz.Jäg.Abt.(Sfl) 643 | 27 | |
| Heeres Pz.Jäg.Abt.(Sfl) 670 | 27 | |
| Heeres Sturmgeschütz Batterie 640 | | 6 |
| Heeres Sturmgeschütz Batterie 659 | | 6 |
| Heeres Sturmgeschütz Batterie 660 | | 6 |
| Heeres Sturmgeschütz Batterie 665[7] | | 6 |

1. Courtesy of Thomas L. Jentz. 2. Includes Pz.Kpfw.I, Pz.Kpfw.II, kl. Pz.Bef.Wg. and gr. Pz.Bef.Wg. 3. Includes Pz.Kpfw.35t, Pz.Kpfw.38t, Pz.Kpfw.III and Pz.Kpfw.IV. The Pz.Kpfw.35t served in 6.Pz.Div. and the Pz.Kpfw.38t served with 7 & 8.Pz.Div. 4. Each of these battalions was to have two companies, each with 25 light and heavy armoured cars of which 10 were to be armed with the 2cm gun. In addition, there were several command armoured cars in the Aufkl.Abt. and the divisional Nachrichten Abt. 5. The third company of each engineer battalion was to have 13 Pz.Kpfw.I & II, 6 Sd.Kfz.251 and 4 bridgelayers on the Pz.Kpfw.IV chassis. Only half of the bridgelayers were issued: 3.Kp. of the Pio.Abt. of 1., 2., 3., 5., and 10.Pz. Div. 6. There was to be one Schtz.Kp. (gp.) with each of these brigades equipped with 15 MTW Sd.Kfz.251s. Each of the sIG Kp. had 6 of the 15cm sIG (Sfl) auf Pz.Kpfw.I Fgst. 7. These Batterie each had 4 Sd.Kfz.251s as command vehicles.

Opposite page: A grosse Panzer Befehlswagen of 1/Pz.Rgt.33, 9.Panzer Division in Rotterdam, May 1940. The division's insignia, a yellow 'XX' can be seen on the corner of the front plate and along the lower edge of the turret side. The vehicle number (103) is carried in unusually small numbers near the upper edge of the turret side. (National Archives, Washington, DC)

Right: A Pz.Kpfw.IV Ausf.D advances through Holland in May 1940. The divisional insignia on the hull front consists of the usual 'XX' in yellow. Few other markings are evident apart from the hull cross. (National Archives, Washington, DC)

# THE WESTERN CAMPAIGN

**Right:** Char de cavalerie 35S of 18e Dragons, 1e DLM. Many of the Somuas from the early-production batches used a vertical swatch scheme as here. The regimental sign, a hippogriffe on a blue circle, was carried on the peleton diamond.

*France:* Bridging sign

*France:* Bridging sign variant

*France:* Variant of 2e compagnie sign

**Below:** 15cm sIG 33 (Sf) auf Pz.Kpfw.I Ausf.B of sIG (Sf) 703.kompanie, 2.Panzer Division during the Battle of France. This vehicle is in overall grey with the battery letter 'B' and the name Bismarck in white.

*France:* Insignia used by 4e DCR, also variant of 1e compagnie sign

*France:* le compagnie, 1e section

*France:* 1e compagnie, 2e section

**Below:** Char Moyen D2 L'Ancre (2028) of 2e compagnie, 1e section, 19e BCC, 4e DCR. Before the outbreak of the campaign, the turret name was probably overpainted with the company symbol.

**Below:** Infantry Tank Mk.II (Matilda Senior) of the 7th RTR in the standard G.3/G.4 scheme. The vehicle name Glanton, the AFV identification squares and the nickname Ali Baba near the driver's visor are all in white. Overlapping the edge of the right mudguard is a small rectangle of yellow-green gas paint. This particular tank did not carry the usual WD serial.

*U.K.:* 3rd Infantry Division (15th / 19th Hussars)

*U.K.:* 2nd Infantry Division (4th/7th Dragoon Guards)

*U.K.:* 48th Infantry Division (1st Lothians)

*U.K.:* 51st Highland Division (1st Fife and Forfar)

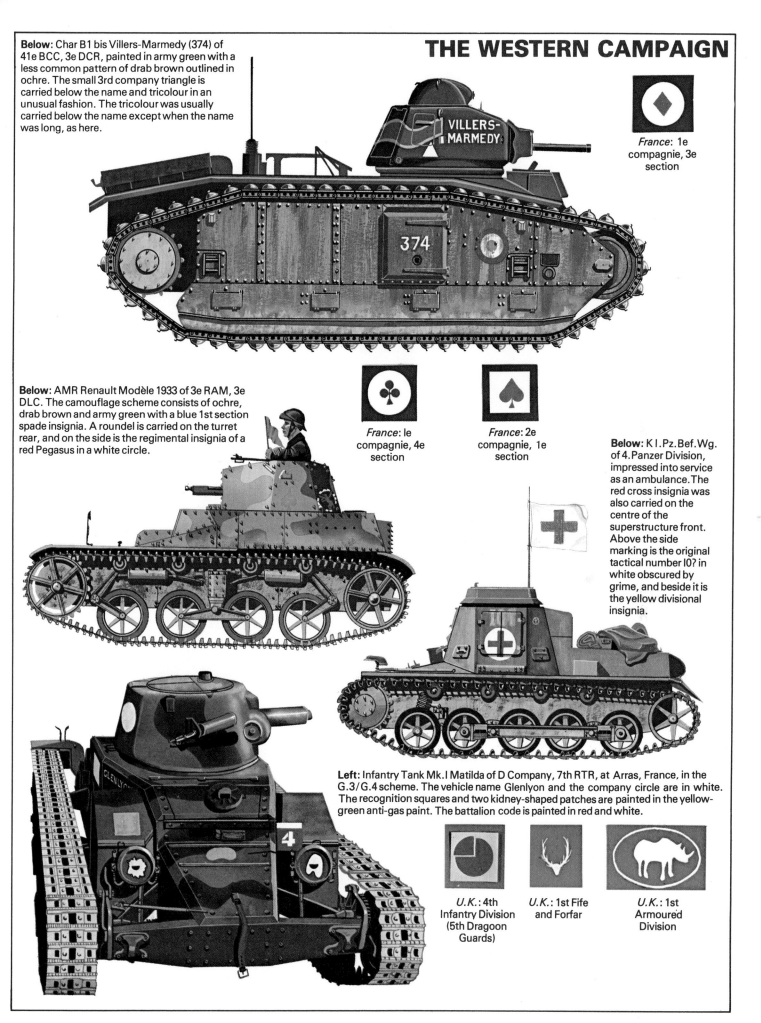

**Below:** Char B1 bis Villers-Marmedy (374) of 41e BCC, 3e DCR, painted in army green with a less common pattern of drab brown outlined in ochre. The small 3rd company triangle is carried below the name and tricolour in an unusual fashion. The tricolour was usually carried below the name except when the name was long, as here.

*France*: 1e compagnie, 3e section

**Below:** AMR Renault Modèle 1933 of 3e RAM, 3e DLC. The camouflage scheme consists of ochre, drab brown and army green with a blue 1st section spade insignia. A roundel is carried on the turret rear, and on the side is the regimental insignia of a red Pegasus in a white circle.

*France*: le compagnie, 4e section

*France*: 2e compagnie, 1e section

**Below:** K l.Pz.Bef.Wg. of 4.Panzer Division, impressed into service as an ambulance. The red cross insignia was also carried on the centre of the superstructure front. Above the side marking is the original tactical number l0? in white obscured by grime, and beside it is the yellow divisional insignia.

**Left:** Infantry Tank Mk.I Matilda of D Company, 7th RTR, at Arras, France, in the G.3/G.4 scheme. The vehicle name Glenlyon and the company circle are in white. The recognition squares and two kidney-shaped patches are painted in the yellow-green anti-gas paint. The battalion code is painted in red and white.

*U.K.*: 4th Infantry Division (5th Dragoon Guards)

*U.K.*: 1st Fife and Forfar

*U.K.*: 1st Armoured Division

**Top:** This aerial view of the turret roof of a Pz.Kpfw.IV of Pz.Rgt.9 shows details of the tanker's uniform. Worth noting is that hatches opening outwards, as shown here, were painted in the dark grey exterior paint, while the interior surfaces of German tanks were painted a light cream colour. (National Archives, Washington, DC)

**Bottom:** There were only a handful of StuG Sd.Kfz.142s available for the Battle of France. Besides the battery number and the stencilled self-propelled gun emblem, this vehicle has had the edges of its mudguards painted white for ease of traffic control. (National Archives, Washington, DC)

**Opposite page, top:** A Pz.Kpfw.II Ausf.b of 5.kompanie, Pz.Rgt.7, 10.Panzer Division displays the regimental insignia on the turret in front of the company number. The platoon and individual vehicle number are carried on a plate on the hull side. (National Archives, Washington, DC)

**Opposite page, bottom:** This schwere Panzerfunkwagen (Sd.Kfz.263) carries a very prominent 'balkankreuz' on the turret side, a practice that became less common after the Polish Campaign. This vehicle was photographed during the assault on Rotterdam in May 1940. (National Archives, Washington, DC)

# THE WESTERN CAMPAIGN

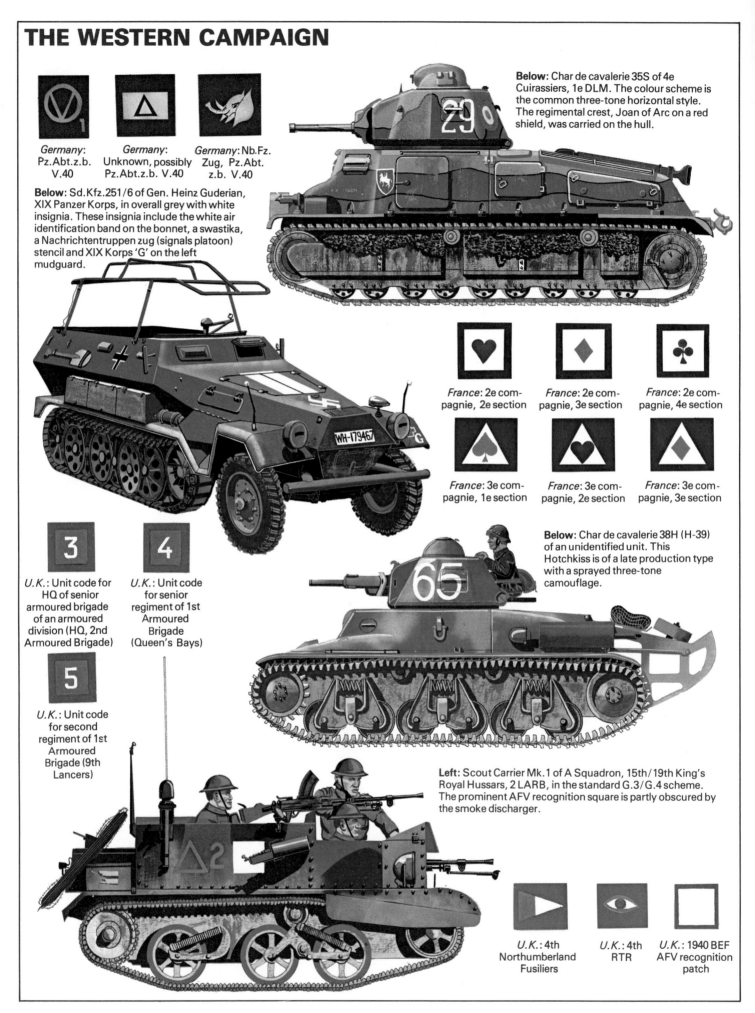

**Germany:** Pz.Abt.z.b. V.40

**Germany:** Unknown, possibly Pz.Abt.z.b. V.40

**Germany:** Nb.Fz. Zug, Pz.Abt. z.b. V.40

**Below:** Sd.Kfz.251/6 of Gen. Heinz Guderian, XIX Panzer Korps, in overall grey with white insignia. These insignia include the white air identification band on the bonnet, a swastika, a Nachrichtentruppen zug (signals platoon) stencil and XIX Korps 'G' on the left mudguard.

**Below:** Char de cavalerie 35S of 4e Cuirassiers, 1e DLM. The colour scheme is the common three-tone horizontal style. The regimental crest, Joan of Arc on a red shield, was carried on the hull.

*France*: 2e compagnie, 2e section

*France*: 2e compagnie, 3e section

*France*: 2e compagnie, 4e section

*France*: 3e compagnie, 1e section

*France*: 3e compagnie, 2e section

*France*: 3e compagnie, 3e section

**U.K.:** Unit code for HQ of senior armoured brigade of an armoured division (HQ, 2nd Armoured Brigade)

**U.K.:** Unit code for senior regiment of 1st Armoured Brigade (Queen's Bays)

**U.K.:** Unit code for second regiment of 1st Armoured Brigade (9th Lancers)

**Below:** Char de cavalerie 38H (H-39) of an unidentified unit. This Hotchkiss is of a late production type with a sprayed three-tone camouflage.

**Left:** Scout Carrier Mk.1 of A Squadron, 15th/19th King's Royal Hussars, 2 LARB, in the standard G.3/G.4 scheme. The prominent AFV recognition square is partly obscured by the smoke discharger.

*U.K.:* 4th Northumberland Fusiliers

*U.K.:* 4th RTR

*U.K.:* 1940 BEF AFV recognition patch

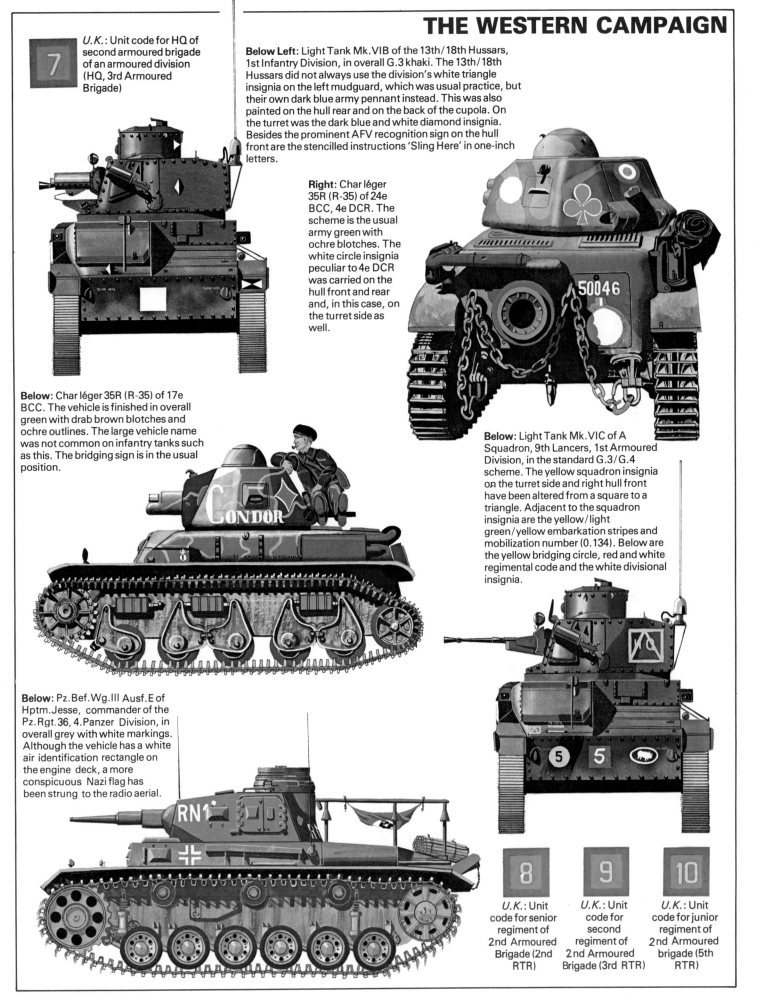

**7**
*U.K.*: Unit code for HQ of second armoured brigade of an armoured division (HQ, 3rd Armoured Brigade)

**Below Left:** Light Tank Mk.VIB of the 13th/18th Hussars, 1st Infantry Division, in overall G.3 khaki. The 13th/18th Hussars did not always use the division's white triangle insignia on the left mudguard, which was usual practice, but their own dark blue army pennant instead. This was also painted on the hull rear and on the back of the cupola. On the turret was the dark blue and white diamond insignia. Besides the prominent AFV recognition sign on the hull front are the stencilled instructions 'Sling Here' in one-inch letters.

**Right:** Char léger 35R (R-35) of 24e BCC, 4e DCR. The scheme is the usual army green with ochre blotches. The white circle insignia peculiar to 4e DCR was carried on the hull front and rear and, in this case, on the turret side as well.

**Below:** Char léger 35R (R-35) of 17e BCC. The vehicle is finished in overall green with drab brown blotches and ochre outlines. The large vehicle name was not common on infantry tanks such as this. The bridging sign is in the usual position.

**Below:** Light Tank Mk.VIC of A Squadron, 9th Lancers, 1st Armoured Division, in the standard G.3/G.4 scheme. The yellow squadron insignia on the turret side and right hull front have been altered from a square to a triangle. Adjacent to the squadron insignia are the yellow/light green/yellow embarkation stripes and mobilization number (0.134). Below are the yellow bridging circle, red and white regimental code and the white divisional insignia.

**Below:** Pz.Bef.Wg.III Ausf.E of Hptm.Jesse, commander of the Pz.Rgt.36, 4.Panzer Division, in overall grey with white markings. Although the vehicle has a white air identification rectangle on the engine deck, a more conspicuous Nazi flag has been strung to the radio aerial.

**8**
*U.K.*: Unit code for senior regiment of 2nd Armoured Brigade (2nd RTR)

**9**
*U.K.*: Unit code for second regiment of 2nd Armoured Brigade (3rd RTR)

**10**
*U.K.*: Unit code for junior regiment of 2nd Armoured brigade (5th RTR)

**Top:** This Pz.Kpfw.III of Pz.Rgt.8, 10.Panzer Division slipped into a bomb crater during the drive into France. The regimental insignia, a white 'wolfsangel', can be seen on the rear of the turret. (National Archives, Washington, DC)

**Below left:** A famous photograph of a Pz.Kpfw.IV Ausf.D of Pz.Rgt.9, 10.Panzer Division. The regimental insignia was obtained by placing a stencil on the vehicle and then spraying around it with light-grey paint, leaving an outlined bison insignia. Below this is a truncated vehicle plate with the front end chopped off. These plates were painted black with white numerals. (National Archives, Washington, DC)

**Below right:** A 4.7cm PAK(t) auf Fgst. Pz.Kpfw.I boards a landing-craft during training in anticipation of Operation 'Sealion' (the invasion of Britain) in the summer of 1940 at Le Havre. This vehicle belonged to Heeres Pz.Jäg.Abt.(Sfl) 643. The battalion insignia, a white Maltese cross, can be seen on the left mudguard. Below the silencer is a stencilled insignia denoting a tank destroyer battalion. (National Archives, Washington, DC)

**Opposite page, top:** A leichte Panzerspähwagen (Sd.Kfz.222) knocked-out by a 25mm battery on the outskirts of Paris in June 1940. Most of the markings have been burnt off, but the Wehrmacht licence plate is still intact on the lower lip of the improved forward armour shield. (National Archives, Washington, DC)

**Opposite page, bottom:** A pair of schwere Panzerspähwagen proceed through a gutted French village in June 1940. These Sd.Kfz.263 bear no markings other than the national insignia. Such a lack of distinctive emblems was common. (National Archives, Washington, DC)

# THE WESTERN CAMPAIGN

**Right:** Light Tank Mk.VIB of the 4th/7th Royal Dragoon Guards, 2nd Infantry Division, in an uncommon G.3/G.4/G.5 scheme. While an unbrigaded unit such as this should have had a white triangle, the cavalry regiments of the BEF preferred less conspicuous colours. On the left mudguard is painted the crossed keys of the 2nd Infantry Division, and behind it on a plate the unit code, a white '2' on a black square.

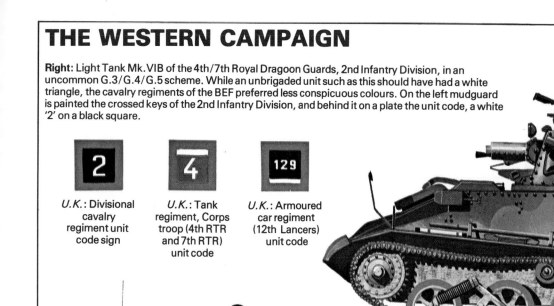

*U.K.*: Divisional cavalry regiment unit code sign

*U.K.*: Tank regiment, Corps troop (4th RTR and 7th RTR) unit code

*U.K.*: Armoured car regiment (12th Lancers) unit code

*U.K.*: Field artillery regiment unit code sign

*U.K.*: Bridging sign for tractor with towed load

*U.K.*: Anti-gas paint

*U.K.*: Bridging sign with weight number in black (Bren-gun Carrier)

**Above:** Pz.Bef.Wg.38(t), Nachrichten zug, Brigadestabe, Pz.Rgt.25, 7.Panzer Division, in overall grey with prominent turret numbers characteristic of this regiment. The signals platoon symbol shown on the inset was carried on the lower right of the hull rear and the left of the lower hull front. A 'balkankreuz' was carried on the upper left corner of the hull rear plate.

**Left:** Char léger FCM 36 of 7e BCC. The FCM 36 was factory-painted in an intricate three-tone pattern as shown here. Note that the vehicle serial is applied over a black rectangle. The battalion insignia, derived from that of its parent 503e BCC, is a stylized depiction of a tank gunner.

**Below:** Char de cavalerie 35S (S-35 Somua) of 2e Cuirassiers, 3e DLM. The scheme is a combination of ochre, brown and army green with black outlining peculiar to many later production Somuas. The 2e Cuirassiers carried no particular regimental insignia.

*France*: 3e compagnie, 4e section

*France*: Pennion of section chief

*France*: Pennion of section sub-officer

*France*: Pennion of 3rd section tank

**Right:** Char léger 35R (R-39) of 3e compagnie, 1e section, 10e Brigade Mécanique Polonaise in overall army green. The Polish insignia, a red poppy on the white grenade bridging sign, was carried on the tool boxes on both mudguards.

*France:* Emergency flag

**Below:** 4.7cm PAK(t) (Sf) auf Pz.Kpfw.I Ausf.B of Pz.Jäg.Abt.643 during the Battle of France. The unit's Maltese cross insignia was carried on the superstructure side as well as on the left rear mudguard. The Panzer Jäger Abteilung insignia (inset) was carried on the right rear hull plate and or the left front differential housing. Beneath the stencil is the Abteilung number. A 'balkankreuz' was carried on the upper left corner of the hull rear.

*France:* 2e GAM (2e RAM in 1940)  *France:* 3e RAM  *France:* 6e GAM (6e GRDI in 1940)

*France:* 4e Cuirassiers

*France:* 18e Dragons (pre-1940)

**Right:** Char de cavalerie 35H (H-35) of 4e Cuirassiers, 1e DLM, in the common army green and ochre scheme with black outlining. The regimental crest is carried on the hull side. The roundels were prominently carried on the front, rear and sides of the hull, the turret rear and the top of the cupola.

**Below:** Pz.Kpfw.35(t) of Pz.Rgt.65, 6.Panzer Division during the Battle of France. This vehicle carries only the black rhomboid plate and, like most of the tanks in this regiment, did not have turret numbers.

*Germany:* Pz.Jäg. Abt.643

*Germany:* Pz.Jäg. Abt.521

*Germany:* 'Balkankreuz' variant, post-September Campaign

*Germany:* Standard September Campaign 'balkankreuz'

*Germany:* Subdued 'balkankreuz' variant during September Campaign

*Germany:* 1940-style 'balkankreuz'

**Left:** A pair of Pz.Kpfw.II of the Aufklärung Zug, Stab, Pz.Rgt.1 near Braives on 13 May 1940. The recce platoon of regimental HQ used the turret code 'R', and could be distinguished from HQ tanks by their higher numbers. (National Archives, Washington, DC)

# ITALY

Italian involvement in the Battle of France was limited to a small incursion through the Alps into southern France, where a solitary Italian tank unit, the 33° Reggimento, saw combat. This unit was equipped with L3/33 and L3/35 tanks.

The L3s were camouflaged in the typical colouring of the period: a base colour of rust red (rosso ruggine) with dark green (verde scuro) blotches.

Markings followed the intricate and colourful system used throughout the war. The basic marking was a coloured rectangle. First company was red, second, pale blue, third, yellow, fourth, green, battalion HQ in black and regimental HQ in white. These rectangles were in turn divided by white bars: one white bar for first platoon, two for second, and so on. Above this was a number in white which indicated the battalion. Finally, on both sides of the rear superstructure corners, the regimental number was carried in white, either in roman or arabic numerals.

# NETHERLANDS

In view of Holland's neutral orientation before the Second World War, it is not surprising that its armoured force was nominal. Indeed, the armoured elements of the Army of the Netherlands East Indies was considerably larger than the force in the home country. The only modern vehicles on hand were 12 Landsverk L-180 and 12 L-181 armoured cars, called M36 and M38 in Dutch service. A further dozen DAF PT3 armoured cars, of indigenous Dutch design and called M39 in service, were being fitted out with armament when the war broke out. Finally, there were five Carden-Loyd Mk.IV tankettes, and a pair of FT-17s, all of dubious utility.

Dutch vehicles were finished in overall dark, semi-gloss green. Landsverks carried provincial serial numbers painted on the left rear mudguard and the front hull plate below the driver's visor. The serial for the M36 was prefixed 'N' (Noord-Brabant province), and the M38 'L' (Utrecht province). Adjacent to this on the driver's plate in the upper right corner was the military serial in black on a red and blue rectangle crossed by a diagonal white band. A two-digit vehicle number was carried in small (7.6cm) numbers on the upper lip of the radiator plate, on both side doors, at the centre of the rear plate, and on both front sides of the mantlet housing. With mobilization in 1939, the civilian pattern-markings fell into disuse. The new military serial was carried on an elongated orange rectangle. In October 1939 a new national insignia, an orange triangle, was introduced.

On the Carden-Loyd tankettes, this insignia was carried on the right of the hull front and sometimes on the hull sides as well. This triangle, in contrast to the aircraft type, pointed downwards. It was sometimes edged in black. The five Carden-Loyds carried names in white on the hull sides: Poema, Jaguar, Panter, Luipaard and Lynx. Photographs of the partially finished DAF armoured cars show little more than the orange serial block.

| Order of battle of Dutch armoured units, 10 May 1940 | | |
|---|---|---|
| Units | Strength | Vehicles |
| 1e Eskadron Pantserwagens | 12 | M36 armoured cars |
| 2e Eskadron Pantserwagens | 12 | M38 armoured cars |
| Depot | 12 | M39 armoured cars |
| 'Yellow Riders' | 5 | Carden-Loyd Mk.IV tankettes |

# POLAND

Although the Polish Army is more famous for its horse cavalry than for its tanks, it had nearly a thousand armoured vehicles at the outbreak of the war. Unfortunately, the majority of these were small tankettes, good for little other than scouting.

Until the 1930s most Polish vehicles were finished in a monotone olive green. The national insignia was a shield diagonally divided in the national colours of red and white. There were no battalion insignia. In the early Thirties a new three-tone scheme was adopted, consisting of small irregular blotches in light ochre, dark chestnut brown and olive green, about 30cm in diameter. These blotches were often outlined in black. In some of the tankette units the colours were applied in broader patterns, outlined in black. To distinguish vehicles within a platoon or company, a system of removable geometric panels was introduced. These signs were fixed on the sides or rear of the vehicle. The shape of the sign determined the company or squadron, while the red geometric design within identified the platoon or section. Some signs had a further design that identified the vehicle. The precise meaning of these insignia has been lost.

In 1936, new camouflage instructions were issued which remained in effect until 1939. These called for a change to a new pattern, with the emphasis on large horizontal swatches of colour. This was accomplished with spray equipment, giving the edges a feathered appearance. The instructions provided patterns for the major types of armoured equipment. Colours used were light grey sand, very dark chestnut brown and olive green. The brown was the darkest shade; existing colour chips look almost black, except in strong sunlight. These instructions were followed closely with few exceptions. In 1939, a battalion of R-35s was received from France, and these remained in French olive green. Similarly, other experimental foreign types, such as the H-39 and Matilda I, were left in their original colours.

The Polish Army frowned on the use of unit insignia, but there were a few exceptions. The two new 7TP battalions had an assigned insignia. The 1st Tank Battalion used a Polish bison in a circle, painted in white or yellow. The 2nd Tank Battalion used a leaping cougar, painted on the turret in white. Some of the lorries of the 10th Mechanized Brigade (10 BK) displayed a red 'centre of gravity' symbol, but this is not

**Below:** A czołg lekki Vickers (Vickers light tank) on parade near Warsaw in the early 1930s, showing the pre-1936 style of three-tone outlined camouflage. Barely evident at the side of the superstructure is a triangular company plate. The colours used in this camouflage were light ochre, chestnut brown and a dull olive green. (Janusz Magnuski)

# THE WESTERN CAMPAIGN

**Right:** Carro veloce L3/33 of the 1 pl., 3 cp., 33° reggimento carristi, in the French Alps, 1940. This tankette is in the standard dark brick red and green splinter camouflage. The yellow and white insignia indicates that this is the fifth vehicle of the 1st platoon of 3rd company. The regimental number is carried on the rear corners of the superstructure.

*France:* 3e section de S-35, 18e Dragons

*France:* 3e section de H-35, 18e Dragons

*France:* 4e section de S-35, 18e Dragons

**Above:** Char léger 38H (H-39) of 2e section, 2e compagnie, 25e BCC, 1e DCR during the battle with Pz.Rgt.25 at Avesnes, France. This Hotchkiss was finished in overall army green and carried very prominent company and section markings.

**Above:** Char de cavalerie 35H (H-35) of 18e Dragons, 1e DLM. While the colours are the usual ochre and green, the turret is finished in ochre and black. This dichotomous scheme usually indicated the vehicle of a regimental or squadron leader.

**Left:** Char léger 17R (FT-17) of 1e compagnie, 3e section, 29e BCC in a scheme of drab brown and ochre. The company insignia was mounted on a black octagonal plate. The signal flag indicates the second tank of a section. The small grenade insignia is without the bridging number.

**Right:** 7TPjw tanks of 1. batalion czołgów lekkich lined-up for inspection in August 1939. By this time, the battalion's insignia had been painted-out. The tankers' uniforms consisted of long, black leather jackets and a Polish derivative of the metal helmets worn by French tankers. For inspection, they are wearing the gas mask bags on their chests. (Author's collection)

**Below:** A parade of wz.29 armoured cars of 11. dywizjon pancerny in Warsaw months before the outbreak of the war. The typical three-tone camouflage, spray-painted in horizontal swathes, is very evident in this photograph. These vehicles served with the Mazowska Cavalry Brigade during the war and, although very antiquated, fought in several highly successful actions against German tanks. (Janusz Magnuski)

evident from photographs of their Vickers tanks. At least one TK unit, probably the 81 dp, used a blue Pomeranian griffon insignia. The 12th Battalion reputedly used a 'puss 'n boots' emblem, but again there is no photographic evidence. Several memoirs mention the use of a red poppy insignia by the 10BK (the commander's name, Maczek, means 'little poppy' in Polish), but it is unclear if it existed in 1939. The unit was reformed as an R-35 brigade in France the following year, during which time the insignia was definitely used, the poppy insignia being painted over the white bridging sign.

Other markings were similarly sparse. Armoured trains had a small, red plate with the national white eagle insignia painted on them. The 7TP battalions had a series of one, two or three stripes painted on the hull sides to distinguish companies, and a horizontal bar below this to distinguish company commanders. The Polish Army was very security-conscious and photographs of Polish tanks destroyed or captured during the September Campaign show no markings at all. It is likely that orders were issued during the mobilization in August, instructing 7TP battalions to remove their distinctive insignia.

**Top:** A samochód pancerny wz.29 in the early 1930-style paint scheme. This pattern was usually three-tone and in the form of small blotches, but in this case brown and green have been used in a more flowing style, heavily outlined in black. (Janusz Magnuski)

**Middle:** A ciągnek C7P is driven onto a self-propelled rail transporter. These tractors, derived from the Vickers 6-ton tank, were used to tow heavy mortars and as recovery vehicles in 7TP battalions. This vehicle is finished in the standard pre-1936 scheme. Many Polish armoured vehicles at this time carried a four-digit military serial, which is evident on the left stowage box. (Janusz Magnuski)

**Bottom:** An anti-aircraft platoon equipped with ciągnek C2P and 40mm Bofors stands to attention. The tractors were painted in the three-colour camouflage scheme, while the Bofors appeared in a uniform dark olive green. Poland built these guns under licence from Sweden. Among their early export customers were the British and Hungarian armies. (Author's collection)

**Top:** A platoon of TKS tankettes practice on an obstacle course. They are all finished in the pre-1936 scheme, although the pattern shown here consists of vertical swathes edged in black. The unit plates, circular in this case, can be seen on the hull sides. Three of these have no platoon designation painted on them, but the fourth has a red circle. (Author's collection)

**Middle:** The TKS and its forerunner the TK were the most numerous armoured vehicles of the Polish Army in 1939. This TKS is finished in the 1936 scheme and has the company designation plate—painted in white and red—attached to the side of the hull. The camouflage pattern, which was applied by airbrush, is very diffuse, making it difficult to distinguish in a black and white photograph. (Janusz Magnuski)

**Bottom:** A formation of 7TPdw and C7P tractors are lined-up for inspection months before the war. The two nearest 7TP belong to 1. batalion czołgów lekkich, as is evident from the circled bison insignia on the second vehicle. It would appear that these tanks are from 2nd company, judging by the two hull stripes on the second tank. (Author's collection)

| Order of battle of Polish Army armoured units and sub-units, 1 September 1939 | | | | | | | | | |
|---|---|---|---|---|---|---|---|---|---|
| Formation | Armoured sub-unit | TK | TKS | 7TP | R–35 | Vickers | FT–17 | wz.29 | wz.34 |
| Mazowska BK | 11 dp | | 13 | | | | | 8 | |
| Wolynska BK | 21 dp | | 13 | | | | | | 8 |
| Suwalska BK | 31 dp | | 13 | | | | | | 8 |
| Podlaska BK | 32 dp | | 13 | | | | | | 8 |
| Wilenska BK | 33 dp | | 13 | | | | | | 8 |
| Krakowska BK | 51 dp | 13 | | | | | | | 8 |
| Kresowa BK | 61 dp | | 13 | | | | | | 8 |
| Podolska BK | 62 dp | | 13 | | | | | | 8 |
| Wielkopolska BK | 71 dp | | 13 | | | | | | 8 |
| Pomorska BK | 81 dp | 13 | | | | | | | 8 |
| Nowogrodzka BK | 91 dp | 13 | | | | | | | 8 |
| WBP–M | 11 sk | | 13 | | | | | | |
| WBP–M | 12 sk | | 13 | | | | | | |
| 25 DP | 31 sk | | 13 | | | | | | |
| 10 DP | 32 sk | | 13 | | | | | | |
| 30 DP | 41 sk | 13 | | | | | | | |
| Kresowa BK | 42 sk | 13 | | | | | | | |
| GO Bielsko | 51 sk | 13 | | | | | | | |
| GO Slask | 52 sk | 13 | | | | | | | |
| GO Slask | 61 sk | | 13 | | | | | | |
| 20 DP | 62 sk | | 13 | | | | | | |
| 8 DP | 63 sk | | 13 | | | | | | |
| 26 DP | 71 sk | | 13 | | | | | | |
| 14 DP | 72 sk | | 13 | | | | | | |
| 4 DP | 81 sk | 13 | | | | | | | |
| 26 DP | 82 sk | 13 | | | | | | | |
| 10 DP | 91 sk | | 13 | | | | | | |
| 10 DP | 92 sk | | 13 | | | | | | |
| 10 BKM | 101 sk | 13 | | | | | | | |
| 10 BKM | 121 sk | | 13 | | | | | | |
| | 1 bcl | | | 49 | | | | | |
| | 2 bcl | | | 49 | | | | | |
| | 21 bcl | | | | 45 | | | | |
| | 111,112,113, kcl | | | | | 45 | | | |
| WBP–M | 12 kcl | | | | | | 17 | | |
| 10 BKM | 121 kcl | | | | | | 17 | | |

| Abbreviation | Polish | English | Abbreviation | Polish | English |
|---|---|---|---|---|---|
| bcl | batalion czołgów lekkich | Light tank battalion | kcl | Kompanja czołgów lekkich | Light tank company |
| BK | Brygada kawalerii | Cavalry brigade | sk | samodzielna kompanja/ czołgów rozpoznawczych | Independent scout tank company |
| BKM | Brygada kawalerii Mechanizowanej | Mechanized cavalry brigade | WBP-M | Warszawska Brygada Pancerno-Motorowa | Warsaw Mechanized Brigade |
| DP | Dywizja Piechoty | Infantry division | | | |
| dp | dywizjon pancerny | Armoured troop | | | |
| GO | Grupa Operacjna | Operational group | | | |

Left: A pair of 7TPjw pass each other during the parade celebrating the seizure of Cieszyn from Czechoslovakia in 1938. This disputed area had been a major source of trouble between Poland and Czechoslovakia since 1920, and was annexed in 1938 after a nominal assault by the Polish Army involving several of the new 7TP units. The tank in the foreground belongs to the commander of 3.kompanie, as can be seen from the three stripes and bar on the hull side. The 2.batalion czołgów lekkich insignia is visible on the turrets of both vehicles. (Janusz Magnuski)

**Top:** A czołg lekki Vickers in the 1936 scheme of sand grey, chestnut brown and olive green. The Vickers were modified by the Polish Army, and the main structural changes to the rear are evident in this photograph. A square, company designation plate with its corner clipped off is attached to the side. (Janusz Magnuski)

**Middle:** Armoured Train Nr.53 'Śmiały' was one of ten trains used in 1939. Like all armoured equipment, it was painted in the three-colour scheme. A small red plate with a white eagle is barely visible on the side. On the afternoon of 1 September 1939 this train helped the Wołynska Cavalry Brigade fight off an attack from 4.Panzer Division at Mokra. (Janusz Magnuski)

**Bottom:** A czołg lekki 7TPjw of 2. batalion czołgów lekkich on parade in Silesian Poland at the time of the occupation of Cieszyn in 1938. The Battalion's insignia, a leaping cougar, can barely be seen on the upper portion of the turret, but the stripes of 2.kompanja are clearly visible on the hull side. (Janusz Magnuski)

# SOVIET UNION

On 17 September 1939 the Red Army invaded eastern Poland in keeping with the terms of the Soviet-German Nonaggression Pact, and met up with allied Wehrmacht units several days later. Among the Soviet units were the 15th and 25th Tank Corps, each with over 600 BT and T-26 tanks. Besides these two units there were a considerable number of smaller independent armoured units, divisional cavalry and infantry support companies.

In light of subsequent political developments, this invasion has remained a source of embarrassment for the Soviet Union and is not widely discussed. There are few photographs of the period, but those that exist indicate that the Soviet armoured vehicles were completely unmarked. They were simply finished in overall dark olive green.

**Top:** German officers look over an FAI-M armoured car of one of the Soviet units in Brzesc after the September Campaign. A year and a half later these erstwhile allies would fight the bitterest battle of Operation 'Barbarossa' in the nearby Brzesc citadel. (I.W.M., London)

**Bottom:** On 24 September 1939, the German and Soviet armies staged a parade down the main street of Brzesc before General Guderian. Here, a column of T-26 light tanks passes a convoy of German lorries. (National Archives, Washington, DC)

**Opposite page, top:** A Soviet BT-7 fast tank drives through the village of Rakow in eastern Poland after the invasion on 17 September. Most Soviet vehicles used in the operation carried no markings and this is no exception, but is finished simply in dark olive green paint. (Sovfoto, New York)

**Opposite page, bottom:** On 17 September 1939, Soviet units poured over Poland's eastern border and attacked scattered elements of the Polish Army. This column of BT-7 and BT-7M fast tanks is seen here crossing the border near Grodzisk. (Sovfoto, New York)

# UNITED KINGDOM

## Camouflage Painting

British AFVs in the 1930s usually were finished in an overall base colour known as No. 23 Middle Bronze Green. In 1939 the War Office issued Military Training Pamphlet 20, 1939-*Disruptive painting*. The camouflage paints were redesignated, the standard No. 23 becoming G.3, or Khaki Green No. 3. The other standard colours were G.4, Dark Green No. 4 (formerly Deep Bronze Green No. 24) and G.5, Light Green No. 5 (formerly Light Bronze Green No. 22). The dark green (G.4) was to be used in equal diagonal bands over the G.3 base colour, with the darker shade predominating on the upper surfaces. The G.4 paint was issued to the troops as a paste that could be thinned with petrol or water. The patterns were not supposed to be identical, and the method used certainly ensured a great variety of schemes. The use of the light green (G.5) was uncommon.

## National Insignia

The AFVs of the British Expeditionary Force (BEF) used no national insignia. However, in October 1939 armoured vehicles were painted with an AFV recognition sign, a white square (about 30.5cm by 30.5cm) carried on all four sides of the hull. It was not entirely popular with the crews, and a couple of regimental histories comment that, at the outbreak of the war, the signs were often covered with mud for fear of them attracting the attention of German anti-tank gunners. According to the recollections of veterans of Matilda battalions, some of the recognition squares were painted in yellow-green anti-gas paint. The units of the 1st Armoured Division seldom, if ever, used this sign.

## Regimental and Divisional Insignia

*Cavalry Regiments*

There were seven mechanized divisional cavalry regiments and a single armoured car regiment in the BEF. These formed into two armoured reconnaissance brigades, but they used the insignia of the infantry division to which they had been originally attached. Unfortunately, photographic verification of these markings has not always been available.

4th/7th Dragoon Guards: Attached to the 2nd Infantry Division, this regiment carried the two crossed keys commonly associated with the division, but without the black rectangle used later.

5th Dragoon Guards: This regiment used the 4th Infantry's insignia, a red circle with the upper left quadrant sectioned off, on a white square.

13th/18th Hussars: This regiment is amply documented in photographs. Some of the regiment's Bren Carriers used the 1st Infantry Division's white triangle marking on the left mudguard. Most of the Mark VI light tanks and Bren Carriers sported a regimental insignia instead. This was a bisected diamond, white on top and dark blue below. Some of the light tanks also carried a rectangular marking which on photographs looks like a white diablo. In fact, it is probably an Army or Corps pennant. The colours, other than the white quadrants, are not yet known.

15th/19th Hussars: Attached to the 3rd Infantry Division, this regiment carried the famous black triangle with inset red triangle on the mudguards of their vehicles.

1st Lothians and Border Horse: This regiment was originally attached to the 48th Infantry Division, at

**Below:** Mark VIB light tanks of the 4th/7th Dragoon Guards at Bucquoy in the spring of 1940 displaying their newly-applied camouflage and markings. The vehicles nearest the camera belong to C Squadron, as is evident from their circular marking. In front of them is a tank named Belvoir from B Squadron, in keeping with the tradition of choosing names beginning with the squadron letter. The AFV recognition sign stands out brightly. (I.W.M., London)

**Top:** A superb shot of the 1st Fife and Forfar on manoeuvres, with Mark VI light tanks in the foreground and Scout Carriers behind. The unit insignia, an elk's head can be seen on the left mudguard of the tank in the foreground. Also evident on this vehicle are the serial number and unit code. (I.W.M., London)

**Middle:** A Mark VIB light tank of 4th/7th Dragoon Guards is recovered by a Scammel in late autumn 1939. The crossed keys insignia of the 2nd Infantry Division can be seen on the upper left corner of the superstructure, and below this is a rather misshapen AFV recognition square. Another such square is evident under the silencer. The black and white civil licence plate is clearly visible in the usual place beneath the rear lights. (I.W.M., London)

**Bottom:** A Mark VI light tank of the 13th/18th Hussars is passed by a French farmer in the Arras area October 1939. On the left mudguard of the vehicle can be seen the white triangle marking of the 1st Infantry Division, and behind it the black and white unit code plate. This tank still carries its civil licence plate on the hull front, and a military serial (T5112) can be seen in small letters on the hull side. This vehicle is finished in monotone G.3 green. (I.W.M., London)

which time it used the unit's blue oval with red diamond and blue parrot insignia. The regiment was transferred to the 51st Highland Division where it used the famous blue square and red circle insignia, with the HD imposed within.

1st Fife and Forfar: There is no verification of the insignia of this unit, but it is believed to have been a stylized elk's head.

East Riding Yeomanry: This unit, part of 1st Armoured Reconnaissance Brigade, carried no divisional insignia.

12th Lancers: No regimental or divisional insignia were carried on the Morris armoured cars used by this unit.

4th Northumberland Fusiliers: This divisional recce unit used Daimler scout cars, which had a red and white pennant painted on the hull sides.

### 1st Army Tank Brigade

This brigade consisted of the 4th RTR and 7th RTR. The 4th RTR used its traditional 'Chinese Eye' insignia on the turrets of its Matildas. This insignia was born in the Great War, when one of the Chinese tank repair men at the depot in Teneur had asked : "If tank have no eye, how can see?" The 7th RTR Matildas carried no distinctive unit insignia.

### 1st Armoured Division

The AFVs of the 1st Armoured Division carried the traditional white bison insignia inside a white oval. There was no black background to this insignia as there would be in later years.

## Tactical Insignia

### Unit signs

Unit code signs were adopted at the outbreak of the war instead of the pre-war custom of painting the unit's name on AFVs. These signs consisted of a coloured block with a white number on it. The sign was sometimes painted directly on the armour at the front and rear of the vehicle, or it was painted on a removable metal plate. Non-divisional troops had a white bar added to the square, either above, to indicate Corps troops, or below, to indicate Army troops. Some of the more relevant codes for armoured vehicles of the BEF were:

| Colour | Number | Unit |
|---|---|---|
| Black | 2 | Divisional Cavalry Regiments |
| Red | 15 | Senior Infantry Regiment Carrier Platoon |
| Black [1] | 129 | 12th Royal Lancers |
| Red/Blue | 25 | 2nd Field Regiment, RA |
| Red [2] | 4 | 4th RTR, 7th RTR |
| 1st Armoured Division: | | |
| Red | 3 | HQ, 2nd Armoured Brigade |
| Red | 4 | Queen's Bays |
| Red | 5 | 9th Lancers |
| Red | 6 | 10th Hussars |
| Green | 7 | HQ, 3rd Armoured Brigade |
| Green | 8 | 2nd RTR |
| Green | 9 | 3rd RTR |
| Green | 10 | 5th RTR |

1. With white bar below. 2. With white bar above.

### Squadron and company signs

Since 1929, British tanks had been painted with geometric symbols to indicate the position of a vehicle within a battalion or regiment. Two systems dating from 1931 and 1939 were in use prior to the Battle of France, but in 1940 the following were the most common.

| Sign | Company or squadron |
|---|---|
| Hollow diamond | Regimental or battalion HQ |
| Hollow triangle | A |
| Hollow square | B |
| Hollow circle | C |

These signs were painted in colour for brigaded units, and those for unbrigaded units such as the divisional cavalry regiments were supposed to be white. The colours were: Senior Regiment, red; Second Regiment, yellow; Third Regiment, blue.

**Left:** A Mark VIB light tank of the 13th/18th Hussars shows the markings used at the time of the Battle of France. The white recognition squares are visible on the lower bow and turret rear, and the regiment's bisected diamond insignia can be seen on the glacis plate and the turret side. On the rear of the cupola is a white Army pennant. (National Archives, Washington, DC)

**Top:** A Cruiser Mark III abandoned near the railway yard in Calais. This tank belonged to HQ Squadron of 3rd RTR, and the squadron sign, a yellow square with the letters 'HQ' inside, can be seen on the turret side and front. (National Archives, Washington, DC)

**Bottom:** A group of Morris armoured cars take part in a demonstration with a neighbouring French cavalry unit near Avesnes in the autumn of 1939. The vehicle in the foreground belongs to A Squadron of the 12th Lancers and is named Arravale, painted in red letters just behind the door. The AFV recognition sign is carried on the turret side, and the unit code, a white 129 on a black square with a white bar, is on the right mudguard. In the background can be seen a French Somua S-35 tank. (I.W.M., London)

| Unit | Mk.VI | Matilda | Matilda II | Cruiser Tank | Carrier | Daimler | Morris | Guy |
|---|---|---|---|---|---|---|---|---|
| 4th/7th Dragoon Guards | 28 | | | | 44 | | | |
| 5th Dragoon Guards | 28 | | | | 44 | | | |
| 13th/18th Hussars | 28 | | | | 44 | | | |
| 15th/19th Hussars | 28 | | | | 44 | | | |
| 1st Lothians | 28 | | | | 44 | | | |
| 1st Fife and Forfar | 28 | | | | 44 | | | |
| East Riding Yeomanry | 28 | | | | 44 | | | |
| 12th Lancers | | | | | | | 38 | |
| 4th Northumberland Fusiliers | | | | | | 12 | | |
| 4th RTR | 5 | 50 | | | 8 | | | |
| 7th RTR | 7 | 27 | 23 | | 8 | | | |
| 1st Armoured Division | 134 | | | 150 | 15 | 30 | | |
| No.3 Air Mission Phantom | | | | | | | | 6 |

**Order of battle of the armoured units of the British Expeditionary Force, 10 May 1940**

These figures do not include Carriers belonging to the infantry divisions. Each infantry division had an establishment strength of 96 Carriers.

**Left:** Crews of the 4th RTR service their Matilda Is during the Phoney War period. The Battalion's famous 'Chinese Eye' insignia can be seen on the upper edge of the turret above the smoke discharger mount. The vehicle name (Dreadnought and Dolphin), red and white unit code, and black and white civil licence plate appear on the hull front. The vehicles had been camouflaged shortly before this photograph was taken, and some of the chalk lines used to mark the patterns are still visible. (I.W.M., London)

**Below:** A Matilda I of the 4th RTR on exercise near Hebuterne in early spring 1940. In this rear view can be seen the square AFV recognition sign carried on both turret rear and on the engine deck, and behind these the unit code and the civil licence plate. (I.W.M., London)

**Top:** A disabled Scout Carrier, believed to be from 1st Armoured Division. At the front of the side plate is a coloured triangle with a white '3' in the centre, adjacent to a white War Department serial (also carried on the rear) and finally the vehicle name. The triangle is repeated on the right rear hull. (National Archives, Washington, DC)

**Middle:** A column from 1st Armoured Division going into action near Quesnoy on 30 May 1940. The only marking visible on the Daimler Scout Car is the WD serial F9420. The Mark VI has the unit code '7' of the 3rd Armoured Brigade's HQ, while the Cruiser in front belongs to B Squadron of 5th RTR. (I.W.M., London)

**Bottom:** A column of Daimlers of the 4th Northumberland Fusiliers. The unit insignia, a red and white pennion, is barely evident on the hull side above the WD numbers. On the rear is a circular blotch of anti-gas paint, and on the rear of the engine deck is the vehicle name. (I.W.M., London)

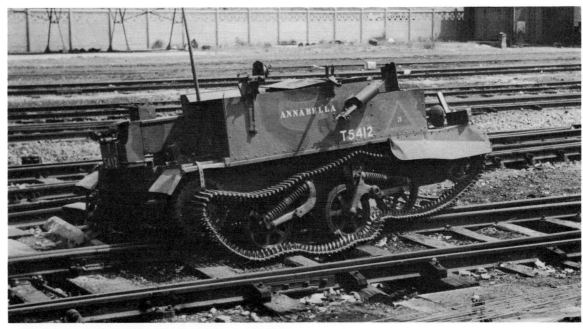

In fact, these rules were frequently amended in the field. The cavalry regiments almost invariably used coloured signs which, in some cases, were used to distinguish squadrons rather than regiments or companies. For example, this was the practice in the 1st Lothians. In some units the rules were ignored outright, as in the case of the 5th RTR which used purple for their insignia. The 7th RTR used the older 1939 pattern signs, which were solid white rather than hollow. Whether 1939 or 1940 pattern, the squadron or company number was supposed to be painted inside in black, though often the regimental colour was used.

### Licences
Many of the armoured vehicles of the BEF retained their civilian licence plates, which were black enamel plates with letters and numbers in white. Besides these, the War Department numbers were painted on the hull in small (2.5cm) letters. These serials were prefixed by 'T' for tanks and 'F' for armoured cars.

## Names
It was the tradition to name tanks and, on occasion, armoured cars and Bren Carriers, though the practice was not universal. Usually, the first letter of the name corresponded to the squadron letter or, in the case of the numbered battalions, with the appropriate letter, such as Demon for 4th RTR or Glenlyon for 7th RTR. In some units the names followed a common theme; the 4th/7th Dragoon Guards, for example, used the names of famous steeplechasers, as would befit a cavalry unit.

## Miscellaneous Markings
Some vehicles had small stencilled instructions, such as 'Sling Here', painted on. Another frequent marking was a blotch of yellow-green anti-gas paint. This paint discoloured when exposed to gas and the blotch was painted where it could be seen easily. Unit commanders were supposed to fly a small coloured flag from their aerials. Battalion commanders were to use a rectangular-shaped flag; section commanders, a triangular-shaped flag; and company commanders, a pennant-shaped flag (rectangular with a triangular cut-out at the trailing edge). Battalion commanders were to use Corps colours with the battalion number on it, while the other colours were as follows: 1, 4, 7 Sections and A Company, red; 2, 5, 8 Sections and B Company, yellow; 3, 6, 9 Sections and C Company, blue.

Mobilization numbers and embarkation stripes were painted on armoured vehicles in transit to France in 1939 and 1940. Each unit was given a four-digit code, painted in small white numbers. Below this were three coloured stripes, each 20.3cm by 5.1cm. The colour of these stripes would depend on the four-digit unit serial. The uppermost and lowermost stripes were derived from the third digit of the four-digit code, and the middle stripe was derived from the last digit. As an example, the code for the 3rd RTR was 0042. Therefore, the third digit being 4, the upper and lower stripes were light green, and the last digit being 2, the middle stripe was blue.

| | |
|---|---|
| 1—Red | 6—Buff |
| 2—Blue | 7—Red oxide |
| 3—Yellow | 8—Service colour |
| 4—Light green | 9—White |
| 5—Grey | 0—Brown |

Many units sent to France in 1939 had these markings removed by 1940, while other units, such as the 1st Armoured Division which arrived later still, would bear them during the fighting in 1940.

**Opposite page, top:** A Bren Carrier nicknamed Hitler's Bogey traverses rough terrain near the Arras-Douai road on 16 October 1940. This Carrier belongs to the 4th Brigade of the 2nd Infantry Division and carries the Division's crossed keys insignia on the left mudguard. On the right mudguard are three coloured bands of the embarkation marking, and near them is the unit code, a white '15' on a red square. (I.W.M., London)

**Opposite page, bottom:** A group of Light Dragon Mark IIIs belonging to the 2nd Field Regiment, 2nd Corps take up positions near La Bassée in the autumn of 1939. On the front plate can be seen the civil licence and AFV recognition square. On the glacis is the blue, red and white unit code, and on the mudguard the yellow bridging circle. The number 6/3 indicates the bridge weight of the Dragon when towing 18/25 pdrs, or when travelling without a load. (I.W.M., London)

**Top:** A Cruiser Mark IA CS abandoned after losing a track during the fighting near the docks at Calais. This tank belonged to the HQ of A Squadron, 3rd RTR. The squadron insignia, a yellow triangle, can be seen on the turret front and side. On the hull front can be seen the bridging circle and unit code. (National Archives, Washington, DC)

**Middle:** This Cruiser Mark IV penetrated German lines near Quesnoy on 30 May and, after causing a great deal of trouble, was finally hit six times. The crew, belonging to A Squadron of the Queen's Bays, managed to escape. A red squadron insignia is distinguishable on the turret front. On the front of the hull, adjacent to the driver's position, can be seen a three-colour embarkation stripe, and on the bow is a unit code consisting of a white '4' on a red square. (I.W.M., London)

**Bottom:** A Matilda, named Gloucester, of 7th RTR after it had been scuttled and spiked by its crew. The entire front of the driver's area appears to be painted in yellow-green anti-gas paint. On the mudguard is the quip 'Heil Fritz'. The tank name and WD serial are obscured by burn marks caused when the tank was soaked with petrol and set alight. (Author's collection)

# SELECT BIBLIOGRAPHY

Besides listing several of the major studies on vehicle markings in the 1939-40 period, the aim of this Bibliography is to provide modellers with a handy guide to some of the more useful articles that have appeared in enthusiast publications. Special emphasis has been given to articles where detailed markings information was provided, or where accurate scale plans were printed. Many of the standard reference sources, such as the Bellona plans, the Squadron Signal In Action books and the Profiles, have not been listed since they are well known and need not be repeated.

## Belgium

Champagne, Jacques. *Les vehicules blindés a L'Armée Belge*. Everling, Arlon, Belgium 1973
Zaloga, S. 'Belgian Armor in the 1940 Campaign'. *AFV News*: Vol.11 No.1

## France

Alazet, R. *Somua S.35. Maquettisme-IPMS*, France: No.7
Hundelby, M. 'Chenilette Lorraine 37L in 1/76'. *Tankette*: Vol.5 No.6
Tavard, C-H. 'Les Chars Légers de Cavalerie H35 et H39'. *BAM*: July 1970
Touzin, P. *Les Engins Blindés Français 1920-45 Vol.1*. SERA, Paris, 1976
Zadziuk, S. and Clark, E. 'The Char B1'. *Tankette*: Vol.13 No.5
Zaloga, S. 'Modeling the R-35 in 1/76'. *Airfix*: April 1976
   'Char léger 1935 R'. *AFV News*: Vol.7 No.4
   'The Hotchkiss H-35/39'. *AFV News*: Vol.12 No.6
   'The Char B1'. *AFV News*: Vol.8 No.5
   'The Char B1 and Char B1 bis in 1/35'. *Military Journal*: Vol.2 No.2

## Germany

Boyce, A. 'Adler Standard 6 Panzer Nachbildung in 1/76'. *Tankette*: Vol.11 No.6
   'Pz.Kpfw.1 Ausf.A and Ausf.B in 1/76'. *Tankette*: Vol.11 No.4
Chamberlain, P., Doyle, H. and Jentz, T. *Encyclopedia of German Tanks of World War Two*. Arms and Armour Press, London, 1978; Arco, New York, 1978.
Clark, E. 'The SdKfz 10 in 1/76'. *Tankette*: Vol.8 No.6
Cobb, S. R. 'The Pz.Kpfw.II, Ausf.D in 1/35'. *AFV-G2*: Vol.5 No.10
Culver, B. *Panzer Colours*. Arms and Armour Press, London, 1977; Squadron/Signal Publications, Carrollton, 1977.
   *Panzer Colours II*. Arms and Armour Press, London, 1978; Squadron Signal, 1978.

Ellis, C. and Doyle, H. *Panzerkampfwagen*. Bellona, London, 1976
Gander, T. 'The 15cm sIG'. *Airfix*: August 1977
Herman, C. *Die 9.Panzer Division*. Podzun Verlag, Dorheim
Hundleby, M. 'The SdKfz 231 Armored Car'. *Tankette*: Vol.8 No.1
Manteufel, H. *Die 7.Panzer Division*. Podzun Verlag, Dorheim
Martinetti, J. P. *Les signes tactiques de l'Axe*. (Document 2) De Bello, Paris, 1976
Reynolds, O. 'Converting the Airfix Pz.Kpfw.IV to Ausf.D'. *AFV News*: Vol.9 No.5
Sauve, J. 'The Pz.Kpfw.1, Ausf.A'. *AFV News*: Vol.10 No.5
Scheibert, H. *Pz.Kpfw 35[t]*. (Waffenarsenal 21), Podzun-Verlag, Dorheim
Sohns, A. 'The Neubaufahrzeug'. *AFV News*: Vol.6 No.2
Steinzer, F. *Die 2.Panzer Division*. Podzun Verlag, Dorheim
Stoves, R. *Die 1.Panzer Division*. Podzun Verlag, Dorheim
Weiner, F. 'Painting of Army Equipment 1939-45'. Translated by D. Filby. Unpublished article, 1957
Wilkes, J. P. 'Early Models of the Pz.Kpfw.II'. *Tankette*: Vol.11 No.5
Zaloga, S. 'The SdKfz 13 in 1/76'. *Tankette*: Vol.8 No.2
   'Modelling the Pz.Jg.IB'. *Military Modelling*: Annual 2. MAP, London, 1975

## Italy

Benvenuti, B. *Carri leggeri, 2/II*. Edizioni Bizzari, Rome, 1973
   *Modelling the CV33 in 1/35 scale. Replica in Scale*: Vol.1 No.4
Pignato, N. 'Mimetizzanioni e contrassegni del RE'. *Notizario di Plastimodellismo CMPR*: N.21, 1978

## Netherlands

Surlemont, R. 'Pantserwagen M39'. *WW2 Journal*: Vol.3 No.3
Vos, F. 'AFV's of the Dutch Army'. *AFV News*: Vol.2 No.5
   'Dutch Armor before 1940'. *AFV-G2*: Vol.6 No.7
   *Pantservoertuigen Van De Koninklijke Landmacht Voor de Oorlog*. (Tank Album Series) Frederick Vos, 1968

## Poland

Cobb, S. R. 'The TK and TKS Tankettes in 1/25 Scale'. *AFV-G2*: Vol.5 No.12

Magnuski, J. *Pociag Pancerny Danuta*. TBU Profile, Warsaw, 1972
   *Czolg lekki 7TP*. TBU Profile 21, Warsaw, 1973
   *Czolg rozpoznawczy TKS*, TBU Profile 36, Warsaw, 1975
   *Samochod Pancerny wz.34*. TBU Profile 56, Warsaw, 1979
Morgan, L. 'The wz.34 armored car in 1/76 scale'. *Tankette*: Vol.5 No.1
Zaloga, S. 'Polish Armour 1939'. *Airfix*: Annual 7 Patrick Stephens, Cambridge, 1977
   'Bron Pancerna 1930-39'. *AFV News*: Vol.9 No.3 and Vol.9 No.4
   'Polish Armored Trains in 1939'. *AFV News*: Vol.12 No.3
   'Organization of the Polish Armored Force in 1939'. *AFV-G2*: Vol.6 No.2

## Soviet Union

Dooley, G. 'The BA-10 in 1/76'. *Tankette*: Vol.5 No.3
Milsom, J. and Zaloga, S. 'Russian Tanks of WWII'. *Airfix*: Guide 22, Patrick Stephens, Cambridge, 1977
Radzievskii, A. I. 'Tankovyi Udar'. *Voyenizdat*: Moscow, 1977
Spain, C. 'The BA-20 in 1/76'. *Tankette*: Vol.8 No.2

## United Kingdom

Ayliffe-Jones, N. 'British AFV Markings between the Wars'. *Airfix*: July 1979
Broughton, J. 'Modelling the Matilda I in 1/35'. *Airfix*: September 1975
   'Modelling the Mk.VI B in 1/35'. *Airfix*: August 1975
   'Modelling the Cruiser Tank Mk.I in 1/35'. *Airfix*: June and July, 1975
Cole, H. *Formation Badges of WW 2*. Arms and Armour Press, London, 1973
Crow, D. *British and Commonwealth Armoured Formations*. Profile Publications, Windsor, 1972
Hodges, P. *British Military Markings*. Almark Publishing, New Malden, 1971
List, D. '7th RTR Tank Names'. *MAFVA-London Newsletter*: No.5
Perret, B. *The Matilda*. Ian Allen, 1973
Weigle, B. 'British Mk.VI B Light Tank in 1/76'. *AFV-G2*: Vol.2 No.11
   'The 1st Lothians'. *Tankette*: Vol.6 Nos.3 and 4
White, B. T. *British Tank Markings and Names*. Arms and Armour Press, London, 1978; Squadron/Signal Publications, Carrollton, 1978

## Modelling

Huntley, I. 'A Question of Scale Colour'. *Scale Models*: June 1975